Untie the Ribbons

Sharon Hoffman

Whitaker House · 21st Century PRESS

580 Pittsburgh Street, Springdale, PA 15144

UNTIE THE RIBBONS
Cherished Gifts You've Always Longed For!

Sharon Hoffman
G.I.F.T.ed Women
P.O. Box 3044
Des Moines, IA 50316

Whitaker House
580 Pittsburgh Street
Springdale, PA 15144

Library of Congress Cataloging-in Publication Data

Sharon Hoffman
Untie the Ribbons/ by Sharon Hoffman
p. cm.
1. Womanhood 2. Femininity 3. Title

ISBN 0-88368-480-2

Printed in the United States of America

1 2 3 4 5 6 7 8 9 10 11 12/ 06 05 04 03 02 01 00 99 98 97 96

This book is for my daughters, two women I admire and who influence me most:

Mindy, whose birth was almost not spared, God knew you were a gift I'd love and need.

Missy, whose passion for life knows no bounds. You bring many moments of joy when I least expect them.

"Every good gift and every perfect gift is from above, and comes down from the Father of lights, with whom there is no variation or shadow of turning."

—*James 1:17*

Table of Contents

Acknowledgments

I am especially grateful...

TO Rob, my friend, husband, and lover. Without your constant support this book would have never been attempted. You never miss an opportunity to bolster my confidence. We will cross the finish line of this race that is set before us. Together.

TO my parents. You two are awesome. Thanks for displaying loving faith to us kids. You are more instrumental in what we are all doing today than you will ever know.

TO Carol Cox. You went far beyond the call of duty, dear friend. Your long hours at the computer and invaluable perspectives added so many skillful touches to this manuscript.

TO Norma Gillming, my mentor for twenty-five years. Thank you for believing I'd have something to say!

TO all the dear women of CCBC. You cheered from the stands and believed in this project right from the beginning. Thank you, sisters, for sticking "closer than a brother" and plugging many holes I could not fill during a busy year.

TO the many women (and men) who will read this book. May each day be a holiday! My desire is that with each gift you open, you might discover truths about yourself that you have never seen before.

"I want first of all to be at peace with myself. I want a singleness of eye, a purity of intention, a central core to my life to help me carry out these activities and obligations as well as I can. I want, in fact, to live "in grace" as much of the time as possible. By grace I mean an inner harmony, essentially spiritual, which can be translated into outward harmony. I would like to achieve a state of inner spiritual grace from which I could function and give as I was meant to in the eyes of God."

— *Anne Morrow Lindberg, 1955*

Introduction

*N*ot long ago, as I was shoving my notes into my briefcase after a conference, I noticed an attractive, middle-aged woman standing nearby. Tearfully she introduced herself and handed me a beautiful Victorian book marker. "Thank you for offering these gifts of hope to us," she finally managed to say. "I've struggled for so long to get my life together . . . now I know how!"

She was right. I know how she feels. I have felt that way before and here is what I have found: With the opening of each gift in this book, incredible hope began to grow inside of me. Hope . . . enabling me to "get it together!"

As we steer fast and furiously into a new century, that heart-cry is being echoed from women all over the planet. By necessity, you and I as women have found ourselves juggling careers, parenting, relationships, and what seems like 'round-the-clock taxi service. The challenge of contemporary daily living leaves us very little time to define what our womanhood actually is. Not many venture to make the claim of "having it together."

As a new bride twenty-five years ago, I found myself in a quiet struggle, attempting to clarify my role as a woman. Can you identify? Believe me, you are not alone. In a culture where roles are so drastically confused, millions of women are longing to know how to become fulfilled emotionally, physically, intellectually, and spiritually.

When I first realized the awesome gifts God longed for me to have, I was trying to find strength to get out of some pretty difficult situations. The contents of His loving gifts of grace held the answers. I still scratch my head in disbelief at how long it took me to open what had been right before me all the time. (I'm not that patient waiting for Christmas morning to come!)

Some of the best times women have together are those chats with a close friend over tea. Let's do just that. Pour another cup and we'll sit down these next few moments together, dear reader, in my favorite tea room opening each package one by one. Let's begin by my telling you how "discovering" them has done more to bring me joy in life than a thousand "how to" books!

Friends began to notice drastic changes in me. They wanted to know why, and how. Over the ensuing months, I began to reopen these truths and principles, sharing with close friends how my life had changed. Very hesitantly, I then shared at a women's retreat what these new insights were doing for me. Whammo! Opening up the gifts in public was opening up me. The blessings spread as other women began to experience the same joys; so I threw caution to the wind, and here I am . . . writing it in a book.

First, I noticed that my attitudes changed. Almost immediately. My family began to change as well. I began to smile. I noticed we began to smile at each other. We had drifted apart and how rare a smile had been!

Now, maybe your husband begins each day leading the family in applause for you, but in ten years of marriage mine never had. My newfound joy had really spilled over onto those closest to me. A few months after my decision to change the course I was on, my husband, Rob, led our daughters, Missy and Mindy, in an impromptu chorus of "We love you, Mommy, oh, yes we do . . . we love you, Mommy, and we'll be true . . . ." Laughter and loud clapping followed enthusiastically!

This demonstration overwhelmed me. I realized how badly I had needed to change some actions and attitudes in my life. When I did, thanks to the discovering of these gifts, I found equally stunning results in the lives of those I love. You can, too!

There you are, a woman, how wonderful! The only one like you in the whole world, uniquely made special and wonderful. Whether speaking out on the coast, mid-America, or on another continent, I've never met a woman yet who does not enjoy receiving a gift. I'm praying that the gifts in this book will trigger in you a new perspective on womanhood. Each gift can help you discover what a beautifully "gifted woman" you are!

Rip 'em open . . . untie the ribbons today!

"If you then, being evil, know how to give good gifts to your children, how much more will your Father who is in heaven give good things to those who ask Him!"
                                                    —Matthew 7:11

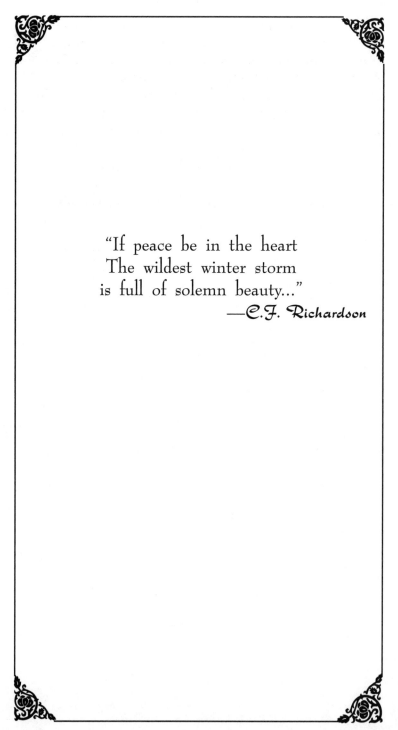

"If peace be in the heart
The wildest winter storm
is full of solemn beauty..."

—C.F. Richardson

Chapter 1

"The Gift of Learning"
Untie the Ribbons of Peace

I can remember looking down at a card table after we had dumped out the contents of a jigsaw puzzle box. Five thousand pieces with corners jutting in every direction stared back. It looked hopeless to me. The first job was to turn all the pieces over so we could identify what color or what patterns were being displayed. Then came the sorting. We'd place the straight edges, which we knew would be the border, over on one side of the card table and the curved edges on the other. Some of our family's most enjoyable holiday times together have been spent in watching a beautiful picture take shape right before our eyes as we "put the pieces together." It was not always an easy task, but the challenge is what made the task worthwhile. We would squeal with delight and a sense of fulfillment and completeness when the very last piece was placed on the table.

Picture your life as 5,000 pieces lying before you on a huge table. Let the pieces represent the many roles in a woman's life, such as family, self, relationships, love life, careers, home — your world. Overwhelmed? Without all the pieces placed in proper sequence, life is just an empty shell. Ultimately, piece by piece, you can begin to see the bigger picture. What a weight will be lifted off your shoulders when you begin to learn how to lay out each piece, placing them God's way, not your own! For years I'd allowed myself to be intimidated by another person's beauty, intelligence, talent or accomplishments which would always result in pain and fear. In order to be in control and make things perfect, I used to manipulate myself and others, but life continued to have its own roller coaster of ups and downs. How could I ever hope for the stability, peace, and joy that I longed for so much?

Before I could discover God's plans for me, I had to relinquish my own. The answer had been right there all the time! It was as though a delivery truck backed right up to my heart's door and dumped nine beautifully wrapped packages of joy and encouragement! Just what I needed to turn my helplessness into health and hope!

I could hardly wait to start opening! Eagerly, I tore into the first box, but the contents were clearly surprising. I figured there must surely be some mistake because I find it second nature to *resist* learning rather than embrace it as a gift! (This "present" would definitely be one I'd like to exchange!) After all, being rather sanguine by nature, microwaveable "quick fixes" rather than lifelong learning experiences seemed much more appealing to me.

Ah, but I remembered my manners. As a child, I was taught that it was impolite to refuse a gift, so I squirmed under the pressure of my proper upbringing and accepted the gift. And I've never been sorry. The Giver of Gifts knew much better than I what would "fit" me best — no need to exchange the contents. I've found that the more I open and reopen the gift of learning each day of my life, the more "peace that passes understanding" results in my heart.

Begin opening this first gift to you today. Learn how very special you are. That is where hope, encouragement, and the will to pick up the pieces really begins!

Feeling Frustrated, Fat and Foolish

I used to be convinced that self-esteem meant "self-improvement." I enrolled in the latest exercise classes, read everything I could get my hands on to develop talents, attended every seminar, workshop, and self-help class available. These methods effectively anesthetized my pains of inadequacy temporarily. Insecurities continued and deepened, resulting only in an oppressive existence by trying to live my life to please others.

The answer came when I changed my focus from self (inward) to God (upward). In desperation, I choked out a prayer. I lay crying until there were no more words.

> "I've been here so many times before. I feel as though I am falling deeper into a bottomless pit. Help me out of this depression, this heaviness. Don't let me go under this time. Please — God, rescue me, love me, help me."

He did! When I stopped struggling. For so long life had been like trying to blow up one of those large inflatable pool toys. I was discouraged just at the thought of blowing it up and then too exhausted to enjoy it after I was done.

One big mistake I made when I was younger was to select someone who I considered to be the ideal woman and set out to be just like her. I began a full-fledged campaign to pattern myself after her walk, her talk, and manner of dress. How frustrated I became after a few days of consistently failing to mimic her style. Sure, I could keep it up for a few days pretty well, but when I would lose concentration, my true self would shine through. A feeling of failure overwhelmed me because I could not be what I admired in that other "ideal" woman.

"How can *she* keep it up all the time?" I thought. She wasn't putting on an act as I had been doing. What I saw was the real person. I was not being the real me. Finally, in extreme frustration, I wailed to my husband Rob, "I just can't please everyone and I can't be like Sue!" (that ideal whom I was imitating.) What a relief to hear his reply as he said to me, "Just be yourself, be who God has made *you* to be." I felt a heavy burden lift when I realized what I had known all along. My identity did not depend on my opinion, or others' opinion of myself, but rather on my being a child of God. I searched His Word and asked God to reveal to me His thoughts, replacing my misconceptions of myself. He answered tenderly, "How precious also are thy thoughts unto me, O God!" (Psalm 139:17).

When was the last time someone has referred to you as "precious?" If you listen carefully to His Word, you too will hear that you are precious to God. Open your spiritual ears and hear! God does love you as an individual. In order for others to like and accept me, I discovered I had to like and accept myself. I would like to encourage you to do the same. You have to live with yourself the rest of your life. You might as well learn to be your own best friend. If you continually downgrade yourself, others start believing you.

I have a dear friend, Jane, who complained about her appearance and often downgraded herself. I thought back to our first meeting. "What a beautiful, lovely woman she is!" But then, week after week, listening to her complaints, I began to find flaws in her appearance as well. I had been pressured into negative thinking about my friend by the woman herself. I had heard her bad points so often I was beginning to be convinced she was right!

Jane, like hundreds of women now, began to open the precious gift of learning . . . those strangling feelings of inadequacy are gone! No more "plain Jane." The results have been dramatic. She has discovered herself and had the courage to change. She has become a new person!

As she told me, "What can I say? Finally, I know who I am and where I am going. My husband is thrilled. There are two things I can never change about myself, but I'm not going to waste time wishing I could. I accept them and am on with the business of living!"

Now, I am not advocating that you broadcast your good points on a billboard or go around in a haughty manner with your nose up in the air, nor am I saying that you should never try to make constructive improvements. However, if there is something about you (as there is about all of us) that you cannot change, accept it and make the most of it by emphasizing your positive characteristics.

There are many things about ourselves we can learn how to change. Some things, however, are here to stay. There is one detail about myself to which I never draw attention. It's never going to disappear, I know I can't change it, so I never mention it or point it out to anyone. I accept it (sometimes again and again) and don't emphasize it. By doing this, I even forget that it exists!

Self Esteem: Buzzword or Behavior?

It used to be common in elementary school for a teacher to drill a truth into a student's mind by having him write a statement on the chalkboard twenty-five times or more. It would not hurt us to write in our journals, "God loves me and so do I." Say it out loud daily. Maybe then we would really believe it!

It is so important to believe that we have value and worth. This begins by accepting what our Heavenly Father believes about us and opening the gifts He offers to us.

The gift of learning replaces past opinions of yourself with the security of knowing what your Heavenly Father believes about you. Can't you almost feel your body relaxing as a spirit of peace stills over you? Let the calmness of His spirit replenish your soul. No tranquilizer, no pill, no coping exercise works better.

"It's Just Not Fair!"

How many times have I heard that from one of my children? When one was allowed to stay up ten minutes longer than the other, or the car keys were handed over to one and not the other — believe me, I heard about it! Sooprise, sooprise, ladies! We must learn that life isn't always the way we want it to be. It doesn't always seem fair in *our* eyes or from *our* perspective, that is. But we must resist the urge to question — because in *God's* eyes all is just and fair. He knows what He's doing.

Attempting to emulate someone else, or "keeping up with the Joneses" is counterproductive. We can all find someone who is smarter, richer, has fewer figure flaws or lives in a nicer home than we do or a zillion other qualities but resist the temptation to compare. Comparing only causes depression. Well, then how does a woman refute the unwelcome yet frequent visitor of comparison? Today, you can begin to win this battle. The hammers of a weak self-image can be so great that even your daily life can be shattered. "We **dare not** compare ourselves with others," cries out 2 Corinthians 10:12. In fact, when we do, we are "unwise," claims the end of that verse. I don't know about you, but comparing my position and possessions with someone else always brings discouragement and discontentment. It indicates a self-centered attitude which leads to my resentment, yes, even malicious feelings toward a rival.

There are times when I have coveted the success, personality, material possessions, good looks or position of even a close friend. Then, in order to compensate my frustrated ego, I made destructive remarks causing conflicts that were sometimes irreparable.

Why? Why me? Why my family? If only . . . . Some of the most pathetic women in the world are those who, in the midst of comparing, indulge themselves in a pity party while blaming God for their status in life. Success or failure cannot be measured by a human. Be what *you* are — what God has made *you* to be. Learn to live with your *own* strengths and limitations. "But by the grace of God, I am what I am" (1 Corinthians 15:10).

Unfortunately, we women depend on each other for our successes to fill a void that can only be filled by our Creator. When past failures, dissatisfaction with personal appearance or bad habits loom so large in our minds, they become the basis of our self-worth. "I just can't help myself," some women say. "That's just the way I've always been and that's always the way I'll be. You can't teach an old dog new tricks." If we condone these conversations with ourselves too often and too long, we find discouragement and defeat beyond our control. But, by the grace and power of God we *can* change. We *can* persevere and overcome! No one is forcing us to keep shifting our feet and sinking in the muck of old failures and discouragements.

Real Women, Real World

Keep opening . . . untie all the ribbons! Discover the delightful peace that comes as a fringe benefit.

Too often our self-image rests solely on our past behaviors, believing the lie, "this is hopeless." It is at that point we become prey to pessimism and a poor self-concept. God wants to release you from these lies and chains that bind so tightly. There can be nights of agony when God seems unfair and it seems that there is no possible way out or answer. Pressures in life often bring need, want, sorrow, loneliness, and unpopularity. Maybe today you are suffering for what you have done in the past; or bear scars because of what people have done to you.

Our joy depends solely upon Him Who said, "These things I have spoken unto you, that my joy might remain in you and that your joy might be full" (See John 15:11, italics mine).

The peace of God, constant and reliable, becomes my joy. Not here and there, bits and pieces of joy — but full, complete. Happiness does not depend on people or circumstances — because those often change. But real peace depends on Jesus Himself. "If ye abide in me and my words abide in you, ye shall ask what you will and it shall be done unto you" (John 15:7). This is what He calls the "abundant life."

Terry Anderson, the American hostage held longest in Lebanon, shares what sustained him during those seven years. "Amid the filth, the beatings, and the chains that shackled me to a wall, I felt so close to the long-suffering Job. I cried out to God with him. 'It's not fair!' God answered: 'It doesn't have to be fair. I'm going to do what I want and you have to accept it.' So it was that I began to learn acceptance." Those 2,455 days of Terry Anderson's captivity found him learning, as Paul did, from a prison cell, "I have learned whatsoever state I am in, therewith to be content" (Philippians 4:11).

As I have my quiet time each morning, I ask Him, "Lord Jesus, guide me in your perfect plan for today." I don't want to depend on my feelings or whether I have slept well or if the sun is shining. If I depend on His sure Word, which is truth, no matter what comes, I'll know it's in His plan. God just wants a willingness on my part — He isn't asking for perfection. Knowing this takes all the pressure off.

Hurting "Way Deep Down"

Today in Colorado, my friend Carol is uncertain about her future. "But how do I get these children to come in for supper? I must be a failure at being a parent. They never seem to obey me. Am I glad I had children? Hardly. I thought having a family was going to be fun, but now I feel like a failure at everything. I hurt so way down deep."

Another friend, Darla, has a severe headache, numbness, and she is in the hospital. "I am not happy with my work," she mutters. "I thought if I got that job it would be the number one thing in my life and would make me happy. It hasn't. My marriage is just a drag too. On our wedding day, I thought it would all be so different." Their divorce is final next week.

In New York this very week, Betty has been struck by the blinding news that her son is gay, and by the time these words are read, he will have moved out of his home into an apartment with his lover.

In California, Connie goes about her daily duties without anyone in whom to confide. She and her husband had felt called by God into the ministry. He later led them to the pastorate. They were burning "with a zeal and a love to serve the Lord. We were bursting with hope, but after ten years, the fire has gone out. There just isn't any delight anymore." Next week, they plan to separate.

The names have been changed, but the situations are real. I share these instances to remind you that *you are not alone*, that many other women are going through severe difficulties as never before. God knows, loves, and cares. But He longs for us to learn to trust Him. I often go to Scriptures that validate how worthy and priceless I am to Him. Those that help me include:

Ephesians 2:10. "For we are His workmanship, created in Christ Jesus unto good works, which God hath before ordained that we should walk in them."

Psalm 139:13,14,17. "For thou has possessed my reigns: thou has covered me in my mother's womb. (14) I will praise thee; for I am fearfully and wonderfully made: marvellous are thy works; and that my soul knoweth right well. (17) How precious also are thy thoughts unto me, O God! How great is the sum of them!"

1 Peter 2:9-10. "But you are a chosen generation, a royal priesthood, a holy nation, His own special people, that you may declare the praises of Him who called you out of darkness into His wonderful light: who once were not a people, but are now the people of God, who had not obtained mercy, but now have obtained mercy."

Ephesians 1:6. "To the praise of the glory of His grace, wherein He hath made us (me) accepted in the Beloved. (emphasis mine).

A great exercise is to go back and personalize each one of these verses back to God. He loves to hear his own Word and promises it will never return void. Read each verse as a prayer. For example, Ephesians 1:6, "I thank you God and I praise you for your glorious grace and especially that you have accepted me in the Beloved whom is Christ Jesus."

Inner Joy Produces Outer Beauty

These verses share the message that I am valuable, accepted, worthwhile, unique, secure, precious and loved by God. He made me. I am fashioned in His handiwork. Let this gift from Him transform your life, as it has mine. You can't help but radiate from inside. The Word, in Psalm 147, shares that He sees me, He **loves** me, He **heals** me, He **understands** me. That gives me hope, understanding and binds my broken heart when I don't even understand myself.

Get to know yourself inside and out. The unknown is fearful to us. It's no wonder women are confused when our culture is always urging for us to seek something "better" or "higher" or "prove our personhood." No wonder we are distressed when we are subjected to unclear standards of what womanhood is today.

We cannot come to terms with womanhood unless we open the gift of true learning. Going to the "world" is confusing. Women have spent an entire 20th century searching for the answers to the questions, why am I here?, where am I going? and who am I? The world does not have the answers, and the result has left women frustrated and confused.

Can you identify with any of these signs of self-rejection?
1. Undue attention to physical appearance
2. Difficulty in trusting God and others
3. Wishing you were like someone else
4. Unresponsive to authority
5. Inadequate self-confidence
6. Becoming very demanding on self and children
7. Unable to accept God's unconditional love.

I talked to a single young woman just two weeks ago who said, "I never thought I could be anything. I wanted to take my life because all my life everybody that I have ever been close to, parents, grandparents, all the guys that I have dated that have used me, ended up telling me that I was a nothing." She believed it and has spent 18 years believing that she was a nobody. Insecurity results when we believe that lie.

As a young girl, my family moved a lot. I didn't have a childhood friend like many do (my closest friend was pretend!). But when I learned how much God loved me and had been guiding me through every move, that brought me a lot of security. "If I take the wings of the morning, and dwell in the uttermost part of the sea, even there shall thy hand lead me, and thy right hand shall hold me" (Psalm 139:9,10). There is nowhere I can go that God will not go with me. Doesn't that bring a lot of security? We have a society full of insecure women who hate God, hate themselves and are fearful because they don't know these truths. They try to cover up, they try to be perfectionists, they try to compensate in many ways. But these ways don't work.

I Was the Ugly, Skinny One

About this time, you may be thinking, "But she doesn't know what I've been through. The rape, the abandonment, the rejection, the cancer, the divorce." No, maybe I don't, but God does. He loves you with an everlasting, unconditional love. When you accept that truth and cling to it no matter what, you will find healing. Begin today to believe it!

For years I believed untruths. I was one of two daughters — I was "the ugly, skinny, dumb one" in the shadow of a straight A honor student sister. I often felt rejection while it seemed my sister was affirmed, welcomed with open arms. These subtle distortions hindered my acceptance of God's love for many years. The enemy came whispering in my ear, knocking often at the door of my mind telling me that I was a nothing!

Martin Luther had it right when he said, "God does not love us because we are valuable, but we are valuable because God loves us." "Herein is love, not that we loved God, but that He loved us, and sent his Son to be the propitiation for our sins. Beloved, if God so loved us, we also ought to love one another . . . if we love one another, God abides in us, and His love is perfected in us" (1 John 4:10-12).

Habakkuk was a prophet of God used mightily in his day. In this book in the Bible of just three short chapters, He shows us how to *wait* for God's timing and *trust*, even when we don't understand. Habakkuk spends the first half of chapter one listening to the world, instead of the Word. He agonized with the Lord, "But, Lord, you don't understand. The people are telling me one thing and You another? They tell me I am a nothing, that I cannot lead, that I am not worthy?" (Paraphrasing mine).

How similar to words I've spoken before! But Habakkuk then begins to listen to God and not to people. As you and I learn to do the same, we can know the prerequisite for loving and leading others. The way to love others is not through loving self more, but to love Christ more.

To be sure, life will bring sorrow, health problems, financial difficulties, and heartache. Through it all, my dear friend, God's love remains. Accept God's love. Love heals.

God - Confidence: The Source Of Self-Confidence:

1. Accept by faith that you are loved unconditionally by God.

2. Take inventory of your personal strengths and weaknesses.

3. Be yourself. Try your wings! You would make a lousy anyone else, but you can be the best *you!*

To accept yourself, you must first be aware of who you are as a member of God's family. That makes you royalty! A child of the King! You are somebody; you were designed for a specific purpose . . . no one else in the world can be you, except you!

To me, that's very comforting. Knowing that God designed me as I am takes the pressure off me. I'm not going to fight His design. I'll change what I can and accept what I can't.

We have a "You Are Special" red plate that we use for family members, friends, birthdays, anniversaries, when daddy comes home early . . . you name it, we've celebrated it! What power there is in reinforcing the idea that someone is special.

The red plate tradition shows honor. It seems to help heal those rejections, hurts, and pain we all have faced. Perhaps today you could share the gift of learning and show honor toward someone you care about to reinforce their "specialness." Convey to them, "God loves you and so do I!"

What a way to influence your world . . . from the inside out! Changed by learning on the inside, now let's have some fun changing on the outside!

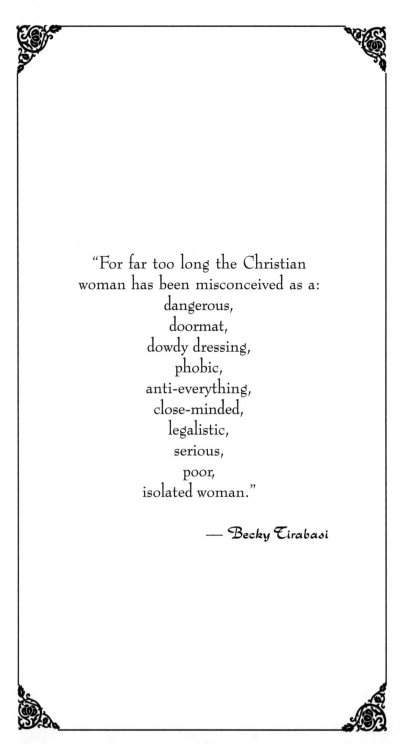

"For far too long the Christian
woman has been misconceived as a:
dangerous,
doormat,
dowdy dressing,
phobic,
anti-everything,
close-minded,
legalistic,
serious,
poor,
isolated woman."

— Becky Tirabasi

Chapter 2

"The Gift of Looking Great"
Untie the Ribbons of Prettiness

Some women are naturally gorgeous the moment they crawl out of bed in the morning. Oh, to be one of those! God forbid that anyone but my husband should see me the way I look before that first cup of coffee and hitting the shower (He loves me very much). My eyes don't even appear on my face for at least an hour after I get up, and then not without liner and mascara. It's pretty scary!

How wonderful it would be to appear at every event flawlessly groomed, not a hair out of place, in the latest fashion, stomach in, complexion radiantly glowing... dream on! While that dream, in reality, is more like a nightmare for most of us, I have not met a woman yet who does not enjoy looking the best she can. This goes beyond vanity, however, to an understanding that our outward appearance is greatly enhanced by true inner beauty, positive self-confidence, and poise. "When you look good, you feel good, when you feel good, you do good!"

Let's target some basic key areas so that we can be the best advertisement we can of God's wonderful care for His children. Pull gently on the ribbons of prettiness and begin looking great today! You'll begin to discover what a gifted woman you can be!

"I'm Not Overweight, I'm Under Tall!"

What kind of program are you on to stretch, bend, stay supple and stand tall? Giving God your body is like giving Him your money — you just cannot outgive God. Give Him your all and just watch your life become a miracle. God used Daniel's obedience in the Old Testament in health as a clear testimony of His faithfulness when we care for these earthly vessels. He also allowed Esther's beauty to be a major part in rescuing her Jewish people! By winning the beauty contest (if you will), she was able to carry out God's plan for her life and sweep King Ahasuerus off his feet!

Fitness does not come naturally to all women. Find a program that works for you! I believe THAT is the key to "staying by the stuff" for long-term results. As a natural couch potato (and the last to be chosen for any athletic event), I got jump-started into fitness when a good friend invited me to begin walking with her. Enjoying the company, conversation and countryside where we walk, I found myself looking forward to the day-to-day energy our walking created. The encouragement of sharing my faith with a like-minded friend makes the hour fly by. We kept each other accountable, which helps a great deal as well. I really miss this time when the cold Iowa days prohibit walking outdoors.

Fitness a Must, Not a Maybe

Maybe joining a health club to exercise three times a week would work better for you. Perhaps a group of gals could meet two nights a week for a workout video as our church group does. Whatever unique twist you can put on fitness that will work for you, find it. That is the start.

Oh, I understand your hesitancy. There's "Miss Body-To-Die-For" bouncing along in front of you in your first aerobics class. You're right behind her barely catching your breath. She knows all the steps and her leotard perfectly coordinates with her shoes, fuchsia socks and headband. What's more, your body resists, with your muscles groaning with every step you take!

So you quit. I know, because that's what I did. I told myself, "you'll never learn the steps, you can't make it, it's too big a commitment, you don't have the time." But, by trial and error, I adjusted my life-style to a fitness program that works for me. You can too. This a perfect time to be honest with yourself. Rather than be a victim of your own excuses, discover activities that you can handle and enjoy. Make a commitment to start. Find a buddy. Start out small so you don't set yourself up for failure. Then as you progress, move forward. A companion by your side is a must for the encouragement necessary to make any physical workout remain consistent.

One great motivating devotional journal I recommend is *Thoroughly Fit* by Becky Tirabassi (Zondervan). This guide is a physical and spiritual workout. It has a companion video for step aerobics. Or, like me, walking may be your energy booster. I'm hooked! And it costs nothing to get going. Because energy creates energy, I can really tell the difference when traveling schedules or weather prevents my walking. An alternative plan is therefore good to have for those occasions, plus the variation in location is a booster, too.

Whatever your preferred choice of workout, try wearing your walkman with tapes of Scripture memory and praise songs to strengthen your body, mind and spirit all at the same time. I have noticed a marked difference in my day when I do. Anxieties are minimized even in the midst of a day full of turmoil after spending an hour transforming my heart and body.

To those of you who are so extraordinarily created that you can eat all you want without adding pounds, I say: count your blessings! But, tag along in this section with me simply because many of us are not as fortunate. We are not the "wine-bibbers and gluttons" nor are we of less virtue. We just can't metabolically "eat like a horse and stay thin as a rail."

The solution is really spiritual in nature. I realize I'm treading on treacherous territory here (since my pastor—husband says it's dangerous to spiritualize dollars or donuts!). But, it does make a difference in a woman's appearance whether or not her heart is Christ-controlled. Christ said, "Lo, I am with you alway" (Matthew 28:20). If we believe that, the battle is half won.

Jesus is not an eccentric. He wants us to look our best. But, we are responsible for what our bodies and faces SAY to those we meet. Our outward appearance is a manifestation of what is truly inside of us.

Choose to Lose!

We had just finished eating lunch and Jan ordered cheesecake, while careful to use a sugar substitute in her coffee. "I lose ten pounds, then gain it back," she complained to me. "I'm on an eternal diet. It's a vicious circle. The worse I feel, the more I eat, The more I eat, the worse I feel."

Our other friends at the table chimed in, "yeah, when I'm feeling blue, I eat a cookie, or a package full!" and "My family doesn't appreciate me so I console myself with eating. The more miserable I become, the more I eat! I've now come to the point where I just don't care."

I know that helpless feeling. When I feel ugly, I become depressed. Dissatisfied with myself. I'd like to escape! One of my easiest and least expensive escapes is a Dairy Queen. The old saying goes, "One moment on the lips, forever on the hips." Apparently, there is no easy answer.

Spiritual exercise requires just as much of "no pain, no gain" advice as does the physical. The choices we make when no one is looking directly affect our testimony when someone is looking. "Well, I was just created this way," is really a subconscious attitude of blaming God for creating us the way He did. God gave us each the power to choose and the only way I've ever been able to improve physically is when I CHOSE TO!

Nail down what it is that tempts you most with your eating. Let the Lord have it! Your body belongs to Him! I have no question in my mind whether or not Jesus overate even though He evidently spent time with people who did. I believe the secret to happiness in this area lies imbedded in the verse, "If anyone would come after me, he must deny himself and take up his cross and follow me. For whosoever loses his life for me will find it" (Matthew 16: 24-25). When you GIVE something up or something away to someone you love, it is different than being deprived of it. Love gives us the power to do this! And a woman's grooming, her adornment, and yes, even her size are definite indications of who is at the control of her life.

I had thought of including some of my favorite low calorie dinner menus, but today we have bookshelves full of attractive meal planning books for you to purchase. I encourage you to do so. Attractive meals take longer to prepare, but are more enjoyable to serve and to eat. Visit a doctor who specializes in weight reduction and consider teaching a class on diet and spiritual principles of weight loss. By becoming a teacher, you will really be motivated and held accountable to what you are teaching. A wonderful Bible study with these guidelines is "First Place." Our women's group at church has used this for a year now with tremendous results.

What a Man Really Longs for in a Woman

We live in a world where breast implants, nose jobs, contact lenses, and tucks here and there are commonplace. What you wear, your body shape, how your hair is combed or what you are wearing are details that are certainly noticed. What attracts the absolute most, however, is the charm of radiance in a woman's face and eyes. Such inward joy shining on the outer countenance is irresistible! You have the power to lift others' spirits and bring sunshine into their cloudy days. There are enough depressed people in the world. Wise was the person who said, "a bright smile does more for the downhearted than does food for the hungry."

I know my husband, Rob, would rather come home to a radiant, cheery wife than the best banquet spread on the dining room table. Perhaps you feel that you are not an exciting radiant woman. It doesn't come natural to you. That is exactly the point. Such radiance and joy can come only from God. Filling your mind and heart with pleasant thoughts, a positive outlook and with Scripture to help you rejoice will keep your countenance cheerful.

Practice makes perfect. Practice smiling in front of your mirror. You will feel foolish at first, smiling at yourself! But don't knock it till you've tried it. While you blow dry your hair in the mornings, go ahead and give yourself a big smile... or just sneak a little one in there if that is all you can do at first. When it becomes natural in the privacy in your own bedroom, you will begin smiling at others naturally when you are out in public.

Laurie attended one of my classes, went home after opening this gift of prettiness and placed smile stickers across the top of her bureau mirror. "I realize this is a little extreme," she said at class the following week, "but I am more likely to start my day feeling kindly toward my family when I deliberately smile the first thing in the morning. I need the little yellow reminders!"

Remember, the more bright smiles a woman wears, the more beautiful and vibrant she looks! The Bible says a merry heart does good like a medicine. I know for certain that my attitude on the inside at any given moment determines how I look on the outside.

Conversely, when I set a positive atmosphere early in the morning, things just seem to start so much better ... for the whole family! If my day progresses with lost car keys, mangled homework and spilled cereal bowls . . . I have already *chosen* to fight the irritability and meanness. The circumstances aren't the issue; my attitude of joy is!

When you look at yourself each morning, do you like what you see? If not, change it! King Solomon captured the idea, "As a man (woman) thinketh in his heart, so is he" (Proverbs 23:7).

Now, don't pour it on so thick that it's unnatural and not genuine. Facial expressions and smiles make you a pleasant person to be around and to live with. Others will be attracted to you because of your cheerful, joyful attitude. Learn to fill your heart and mind with positive Scriptures that will transform you from the inside out as you go through your day. Playing tapes and writing verses on post-it papers placed in my car or desk really has helped me with memorizing Scripture. Prepare your heart with a sense of beauty that cannot help but come across your face. No amount of cosmetics, no beautician or wardrobe consultant can make a bigger difference!

The secret to this beauty regimen can be found in Philippians 4...

"Be careful for nothing; but in every thing by prayer and supplication with thanksgiving let your requests be made known unto God.

And the peace of God which passeth all understanding, shall keep your hearts and minds through Christ Jesus.

Finally, brethren, whatsoever things are true, whatsoever things are honest, whatsoever things are just, whatsoever things are pure, whatsoever things are lovely, whatsoever things are of good report, if there be any virtue, and if there be any praise, think on these things" (Philippians 4:6-8).

Joy is the one ingredient that the world cannot buy. When this quality is genuinely evident, others take notice and want what you have. A man longs for a woman who is warm, who smiles, and who is radiant on the outside because it flows from the inside!

Most of us will not get to do what the Bible character Esther did. She got to spend a whole year of her life beautifying herself with the finest creams, perfumes and oils! But the beauty of a thankful spirit in a very ungrateful world is something each man longs to come home to. Daily, begin acquiring a thankful, joyful heart and commit to focus on the good things that God is allowing in your life rather than the trials. You will be absolutely beautiful when your encouragement is found in the Lord. As King David expressed it, "Thou wilt show me the path of life: in thy presence is fulness of joy..." (Psalm 16:11a).

The couples that my husband and I counsel reveal to us that men would trade any amount of physical beauty in his wife for her to acquire inner peace. He longs to see radiant happiness in her spirit. After four weeks of practicing "the smiling" principle at my ladies' Bible study recently, we wives received positive feedback and affirmation from our husbands. Not only did we individually smile more from a radiant heart, but our husbands began to *smile back* at us! Relationships began to "come alive" as partners responded favorably to the simple stimulus of a smile. (You'll read about more wonderful guidelines to energize your marriage in a later chapter!)

Maximum Results with Minimum Time

A first step in good communication with others is to arrive at any function looking our very best. You only have one chance to make a first impression! Until you can project your inner self to others through conversation, your outer appearance has to do the communicating.

Good personal grooming begins with a means to an end. When you are confident that you look your best, then you can concentrate on others around you. Before people are willing to listen to what you have to offer, they have to first get past the visual barrier of how you look.

Maybe it's because of how I look first thing in the morning, but my first advice is: get decent first thing in the morning! I know many will say to begin first thing with your quiet mediation time, but I always do anything better if I am ready to face the day. And I feel sorry for God having to meet with millions of us in hair curlers, grungy robes, and all that morning breath!

I put on the coffee, shower, and put on my clothes while I'm beginning my conversations with the Lord. Then the stage is set to dress and be at my "appointment" on time with God; coffee cup, Bible, and journal in hand. I have learned over the years not to sit at my desk where the day's agenda is a distraction. Rather, I have chosen an overstuffed chair in our little living room. That way, I am not tempted to stop and clean, organize or fluff anything.

In Proverbs 31, we find the "ideal gifted woman." The indication of the Proverb seems to set a pattern of not overdoing outer appearance, so I don't want to either. In fact, only one verse out of twenty-two was devoted to describing how this worthy woman *looked*. Proportionately, I have desired to find low-maintenance beauty care routines that do the trick, but minimize the time necessary to achieve maximum results. What that means is that out of every twenty-four hour day, I want to give just a little over one hour to my looks. Remember, it's not how long you spend on a task, but how effective you are. Most of that hour is in the morning, then later in the day or early evening I may quickly repair my face, hair, and redress when the occasion calls for it.

"Painting the Barn"

"A little fresh paint never hurt any barn door" is a wise old farm-town saying. Most women can stand some "fresh paint." Using makeup appropriately can be our best appearance asset. Makeup can bring out your best features and minimize your flaws. Just a little cheek blush, eye mascara, and lip gloss to achieve the fresh, natural look accomplishes wonders.

Don't make the mistake of pouring on tons of liquid makeup or powder to cover occasional complexion problems. A face that looks stiff, unnatural, or that rubs off on your husband's coat sleeve when he puts his arm around you, appears ready for a masquerade party. Moderation is the key. No man wants to feel like he's accompanying a clown in costume.

The art of effectively applying makeup is done with discretion and naturalness. Select tones that closely match your facial and hair coloring. My daughters and I have found it a big help and great fun to be "color analyzed" by a professional makeup consultant. Correct coloring is extremely important for it can save you hours of frustration and hundreds of dollars in the long run. My "trial and error" guessing games with makeup used to waste a lot of energy, time and money.

"Makeup and Moisturizing Magic"

- To avoid "ring around the collar," do not apply foundation to your neck. If there is a noticeable line at the chin, go to a lighter shade.

- Add a drop or two of Wilton food coloring (red, burgundy, or a pink) to a pot of lip balm, then apply with a cotton swab. Best lipstick/gloss you can find! (outline lips with lipliner first).

- Never go to bed without removing makeup first (exception would be on your honeymoon!). Sleeping with that dirt and those dead cells will eventually take its toll on your complexion.

- Use an astringent for oily skin or monthly breakouts. Lemon juice also works well to help dry excess oils.

- For a special event or when you feel you need an added glow to your complexion, lightly apply Vaseline petroleum jelly under the eyes and across cheeks. No matter how tired you are, you'll arrive at any event absolutely radiant!

- Always apply moisturizer to the skin right after bathing to prevent the surface moisture from evaporating. I like to heat peanut oil until warm and massage on my throat, elbows and feet.

- To avoid that cracked, flaky look on your legs, always shave after moistening with warm water such as after or during your shower. Apply shaving cream or lotion to allow the hair to become soft and pliant. Always use a sharp blade and shave in the direction of the growth of the hair.

How's Your "Curb Appeal"?

When real estate people drive prospective buyers up to a house, they show the "curb appeal" — how the entire house as a package is displayed. The outer shell you live in is your curb appeal. The beauty of God's woman is so needed in this world. Don't be tempted to let vulgar or immodest clothing taint your body as a substitute for true loveliness.

Of course, it's fun to express ourselves in what we wear. What makes you especially pretty? Take inventory of your closet. Any items that have not been worn in the past year need to be given away. Stand in front of a large mirror with plenty of daylight and critically check remaining items for the correct fit, the right colors, and any areas in need of mending.

How about the total fit? Modesty is the key. Dressing in clothing that exposes much of your bust and legs leaves nothing to the imagination. No wonder our men and sons struggle so with their thought life. In fact, some mothers I know actually encourage their teenage daughters to dress in a way to call attention to herself sexually.

When you sit near a man in a restaurant or at work dressed in such a manner, believe me, he is not thinking about that sales report he has to complete by tomorrow. Virtue and purity are not popular words as we go into the twenty-first century, and there's no one who enjoys dressing the current style more than I do. But, let's remember, we can be guided by trends, not blinded by them. Clothing needs to be a background for you, not call attention to itself.

Because how we look can affect our personal witness of who we are on the inside, I hope some of these ideas will be helpful. Even our shopping trips need vigilance in prayer. I have little time for personal shopping, so when I do shop I am usually on a mission looking for something in particular. My life-style determines needs in my wardrobe. Working in an office in my home now, I have different ensembles, shoes, and accessory needs than I did when working at our local elementary school.

Choose a Family of Colors

Over time, my wardrobing has followed one guiding principle: choose a certain family of colors that are right for me and stay within those hues. That way, if every new purchase I make passes the "color family" test, I probably already have the shoes, jewelry, handbag and layering items to complete the outfit. Traveling is easy because the coordinates combine to make several outfits.

I'm generally a black and white woman. What easier basics to start with? Almost anything I buy, "goes." When I buy a piece that varies from the color family, such as earth tones, which I do enjoy from time to time, I find myself dawdling in front of the closet. It makes it a lot harder to pull an outfit together because I don't always have the foundation pieces or accessories.

This sounds expensive, but over time you'll find the benefits far outweigh the time and money wasted in "mistakes" along the way. The three stores where I know I can find what I need and like have become my shopping mainstays. I have also learned when the best times for markdowns are at all three stores. It is an advantage to your pocketbook as well, to know clerks well enough that they are willing to give you a call when certain items come in or do time-consuming calling around to locate garments in your size.

Everyone can come up with creative ways to accumulate clothing to feel your best. I went so far as to devote a morning a week working at one of my favorite shops for that very reason. With two daughters in college and my own need to update some items in my closet, the discount and seeing firsthand what was in style that fall was well worth it. Missy and Mindy also have me hooked on going to quaint thrift shops with them. Some of our favorite eye-catchers used to be somebody else's treasures. The idea is to look really "together" and "kept" with the most amount of quality, but the least amount of money.

Maybe you're a girl who likes brown! Start today...eliminate all that does not coordinate with your browns, then concentrate on creamy, ivory, chocolates, and gold when you make your next purchase. In the next year, watch to see how much more you are enjoying your clothes.

Five basic items to get you started are:
1. A jacket or blazer
2. Two skirts, one casual and one dress.
3. Two pants, one could be nice-fitting jeans.

To these basics, I simply add prints and solids in various colors to add interest and coordinate. Next, I purchase sweaters, scarves, jewelry and shoes to add variety. Of course, while this gets most of us started, you will want to alter the list according to your life-style and career needs. There are weeks that I practically live in my garden, then there are weeks of traveling and speaking each day. Certainly, each calls for an entirely different look. Dark colors are slenderizing. Choose black, rich brown and midnight navy to minimize heavier parts of the body. If you want to draw attention away from heavy thighs, wear dark skirts or slacks and place the softer colors near the face. Monochromatic styles (one color outfits) have the most slimming, streamlined effect.

Irresistible Beauty

I encourage you to reach your highest potential in looking your best each day. But, do remember . . . life with coordinated wardrobes and carefully applied makeup is marvelous, but unless a person is beautiful inside, all is in vain. Often before I speak to groups, I pray, "Lord, may what I share of your love from my heart be twenty-two times more obvious to these women than how I look on the outside." That is the gift of looking great in correct proportions. No better cleanser, toner or "beauty enhancer" can be found!

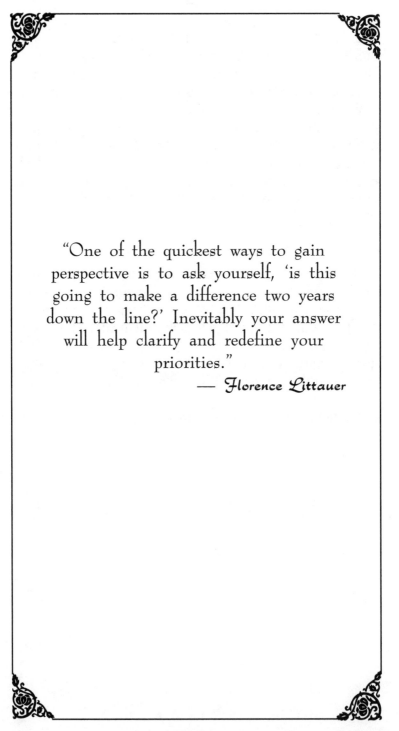

"One of the quickest ways to gain perspective is to ask yourself, 'is this going to make a difference two years down the line?' Inevitably your answer will help clarify and redefine your priorities."

— *Florence Littauer*

Chapter 3

"The Gift of Living"
Untie the Ribbons of Priorities

One of these days I'm going to get organized, we all joke with varying degrees of resolve. We know that life does not always cooperate with even our best laid plans, but some of us haven't made a plan at all.

A good plan begins not with a list of duties and schedules, but with an evaluation of your personal life goals and the goals of each member of your household. Without goals in mind you may find yourself spending way too much time and energy on the things in life that are actually the least important to you.

Help! I'm Drowning in Dishes and Laundry

Has there been a time in your life when you wrote down on paper your life purposes and goals? Dreaming and goal setting cannot be done hastily. At the beginning of my marriage twenty-five years ago, I was challenged to take a blank sheet of paper and at the top of it write "life goals." I had never taken the time to put my heart's desires into words before. To sincerely seek God's will for my life and for His glory helped point me in the direction this past quarter of a century has gone. No, I haven't always stayed on course, but goal setting positioned me to know where I hoped to be and what I hoped to do by the time I end life on this earth.

I want to be like that woman of Proverbs 31:25 as she smiles at the future... probably able to do that because she was a great planner! You know, the longer I live, the more I realize that what is really important in this life is what will last eternally. What I wrote as my number one goal twenty-five years ago still holds true for me: "To make a loving mark on others through my life that will point them to the true and living God." How poignant the saying we've all heard: "Only one life: 'twill soon be past, only what's done for Christ will last!"

What are your life dreams and goals? Knowing where you are going helps put even the most tedious chores in proper perspective. You will begin to sense purpose and satisfaction in your daily life if you know where you are headed in the long haul.

I encourage getting away for an entire day of envisioning and recapturing those "shelved" aspirations. Allow yourself to dream again! You could borrow an empty office, rent a motel room, plant yourself alone on the beach; whatever it takes to give yourself the silence and uninterrupted time for listening to the Lord's promptings in your heart. Be courageous and specific as you write. By putting your longings into words, you will better define practical ways to accomplish your goals. Until I clarified on paper what I wanted to accomplish in my lifetime, I was uncertain HOW to even start!

What a shame it is that we often take greater care planning a vacation than we do planning for our lives! When you take a trip you decide where you'd like to go, what you want to take and how to get there. You check on what provisions you will need and pack accordingly. You map out which direction will be taken, what roads, what means of transportation, etc. Then along the way, if you happen to get off-course you can return to your original plan and personal charting to make sure you get there!

Increased fulfillment and personal satisfaction is what life-planning is all about. Then, when uncharted curves in the road appear along life's way (and they will!), you will be able to refer back to your original goals and go on with new determination. Stephen Covey, author of *The Seven Habits of*

Highly Effective People, calls this a "personal mission statement." He states...

> "Writing or reviewing a mission statement changes you because it forces you to think through your priorities deeply, carefully, and to align your behavior with your beliefs...you have a sense of mission about what you're trying to do and you are excited about it."

That's exactly how I began to feel! I became motivated in my relationships, writing and speaking because I had a target to aim for! By an act of your will today, you can begin to identify YOUR answers to the "what am I doing here? where am I going?" questions of life. People without a plan are just wandering aimlessly ... and it shows in everything they do. Those who chart a course become keenly aware of God's placing them here on this earth for a purpose. They begin to make improvements in needed areas of their lives and GROW to reach their potential in talents, character strengths, and accomplishments. With goals, little by little we begin to take responsibility for increased effectiveness in our lives!

"I Have a Dream..."

Essentially, it is an exercise in imagination — much like a little girl who dreams about what she'd like to be "when she grows up." If that question were posed to a classroom of first-graders, they would have no trouble coming up with a myriad of answers immediately. They love to imagine! Everything from "firefighter to animal trainer" and "a mommy to McDonald's worker" would be mentioned. Children are great at dreaming! We should never lose the art.

When is the last time you dreamed? Or really believed in what God could do in and through you to touch others' lives? Allow yourself today to begin visualizing yourself as a more effective parent, pursuing a dream deferred, going back to school, entering a more challenging career or taking on a leadership position that requires more responsibility. Dare to live outside of the narrow script you have written far too long for yourself!

The rewarding results speak for themselves! For years I have challenged women in my classes to set long-range and short-term goals. The long-range goals are what you want to accomplish in a year, in ten years, in a lifetime. The short-term goals are the day-to-day and weekly goals. Women have written months later to exclaim the positive changes in their capabilities and self-esteem. Accomplishments have far exceeded their hopes and dreams! They have expanded to tackle new horizons, their daily scheduling has become profitable, and their husbands are thrilled at their new perspective of life overall.

God longs for us to get a biblical picture of priorities so that we can have HOPE and not a defeated spirit with each new day. "I know the plans that I have for YOU, plans for welfare and not for calamity, to give YOU a future and a hope" (Jeremiah 29:11).

Jesus himself had a life goal on this earth which was... "to seek and to save that which was lost" (Luke 19:10). This gave much urgency to His decision making, scheduling, and planning. It can do the same for each of us. One-half of me fears rigidity and would love to leave my daytimer open-ended with each square blank.... just to see what the day brings! The other half of me craves the security that measurable time management brings. But I know from experience the marvelous results from goal-setting and priority-planning.

Your "mission statement" will remind you:

- What is important in life
- What values you believe in
- How you want to spend your time daily
- Where you are ultimately headed
- Who is ultimately "in charge" of your life!

Go for it! Go alone to a secluded place or at least draw the blinds, take the phone off the hook awhile and before the Lord, ask Him to help you know your own heart longings. Try a few rough drafts, then after some rewording and rethinking

... you will have it! Write your yearnings on an index card and post it where you can regularly review it as a reminder of Who and what you are striving to live for. I have mine in my yearly prayer journal to regularly review and keep myself on track. Now for you cheaters ...be sure to write them ... or you won't reach them!

Time to Share and Spare

We do not all have the same amount of material resources, but we all have the same number of hours in each day. The very best gift I can give myself or my family is spelled TIME. In our ever-changing world, "home" needs to be more than just a place to lay our heads and grab our meals. For most of us, it represents stability, comfort and security. It means a place we can come to where we are accepted just as we are and where we can be ourselves. But it takes more than just hanging a cross-stitched "Home Sweet Home" plaque on the wall to make a house a home.

To make a home a really special place takes work and commitment and planning. For the most part, yes, even as we begin the 21st Century, the duties of managing a home fall squarely on the shoulders of the woman of the house. Entering marriage and ministry at the same time, as a new bride I devoured everything in print on the subject of home management . With our hectic schedules, yet wanting to be available to Rob, I knew I needed a "plan"! Our tiny three-room apartment has grown into a four-bedroom house. Now Rob has responsibilities as the Senior Pastor, ... and I really need to be organized!

How about you? Feeling swamped with all you are juggling? It can be quite a balancing act if you don't have a feasible plan. I use the plan that Ivy Lee, a management consultant, devised. When I began to integrate each step of this "Twenty-Five Thousand Dollar Plan" each day, I found myself to be calmer, unrushed, and accomplishing more than ever! By the way, Ivy Lee received twenty-five thousand dollars for suggesting these principles to the president of his company! And believe me, it is worth every cent when applied to household management as well.

The Twenty Five Thousand Dollar Plan

- Every night write down the important things you need to get accomplished the next day.

- Number them in order as to importance (i.e. dental appointment, vacuum, etc.).

- The next day, finish as much on your plan as is possible. Do the hardest tasks first.

- When interruptions come, accept them, then go right on finishing each item.

This plan of organization will enable you to go out when your husband suggests dinner out unexpectedly or your child calls and the tennis shoes must be rushed to the school "NOW!" You will be calm and unrushed, because you will have had your most important jobs completed. You're using a plan!

With this new feeling of accomplishment you will even have pampering time for yourself. Each day, schedule in one fifteen minute period for yourself. You will be able to keep your nails groomed, brush your hair to a healthy glow, bask in the sun for an afternoon rest or soak in a warm bubble bath.

Years ago in college, my roommates and I used to enjoy a fifteen minute nap with our feet elevated on a pillow before an important date. I had forgotten that beauty tip until recently. It still works! I try to prescribe one for myself daily and usually schedule it right into my $25,000 Plan. Besides renewed energy and strength, it returns sparkle to tired eyes. So stretch out and revitalize.

The Bible says that... "a merry heart doeth good like a medicine" (Prov. 17:22). When I am rested, my heart can be much merrier. Sometimes the most "spiritual" thing I can do is take a nap.

Subject to Change

I wanted to cry. It was one of "those" days. My best laid

plans were scrapped by interruption after interruption. I was about seven years behind in my ironing. Missy and Mindy were both clamoring for my attention. I had accidentally driven away from the store without remembering to drive through for my groceries. The cleaners had lost Rob's favorite shirt. I was going under for the third time. By noon, I was disgusted, discouraged, and just about defeated. But I determined to have a "merry heart"... even if it killed me.

It just about did. By the time Sandy, our small poodle, had squirmed out of the backyard fence and returned at the front door muddy and dripping wet, I knew I had two choices; go bananas or be flexible. I then had to adjust to Plan B or Plan C or even T! My day was salvaged when I remembered I set the atmosphere for everyone in my home, so instead of crying, I laughed rather hysterically.

Missy and Mindy began to laugh. The neighbor girl who found Sandy laughed with us. A merry heart melts away the troubles. Somehow it helps when we can laugh at ourselves, at all the crazy quirks in even the best laid plans. What fun we had that evening at supper time retelling our day, not as a tragedy, but as humorous.

I like the quote "I was an oak. Now I'm a willow, I can bend," by Buffy St. Marie. I can claim the verse, "This is the day which the Lord hath made; we will rejoice and be glad in it" . . . no matter what! (Psalm 118:24).

Remember, when things go wrong, and they will, only your plan has failed; *you* haven't.

Pace yourself. Do not put on tomorrow's plan everything you should have been doing for the last six months. You can't move a mountain in one day. "Spring cleaning" is not one item — nor a way to balance your list. Be realistic. Women who are used to killing themselves to keep up with the superwoman image tend to burn out on this plan quickly. For two weeks, faithfully use the Twenty-Five Thousand Dollar Plan and watch your calendar begin to be your friend rather than your worst enemy.

Our greatest asset with the $25,000 Plan is our individuality. Learn your particular ebb and flow of energy levels, family obligations, daily aspirations, responsibilities and talents. All of these factors go into the making of a balanced equation where time management is concerned. Several things to remember as you start:

1. **Set your time with the Lord daily as an "appointment."** I have found that setting a specific time and place rather than "working in" my quiet time, keeps me accountable! If I have actually filled a time slot for my time with the Lord, and one of us does not show up ... it won't be Him!

2. **Be open to new ideas.** Office managers are constantly changing procedures to increase productivity. Read home management books (several good ones are listed at the end of this chapter) and attend workshops, classes, or anything that helps your skills.

3. **Communicate effectively with those you lead/manage.** Take time to communicate with family members to coordinate plans, cars, schedules, and goals of the day with each other. This saves a lot of frustration later ... on everybody's part!

4. **Prioritize.** Know how much time each job should take. Are clean windows really worth three hours seeing that your child is in a play performance four nights this week? I streamline tasks during hectic weeks. If something can wait or if I can delegate the job, it's worth it to me to keep the family running smoothly.

5. **Good managers fill their homes with the proper equipment necessary to do the job effectively.** Look at your supplies. Put more efficient equipment into the budget — they will be the most important pieces you buy!

6. **Make your home work for you. Set up your own "nerve center."** Organization needs a station, whether it is a complete room made into your office or a desk of your own in the corner of the kitchen. This is a must to keep files, phone numbers, papers, correspondence, and coordinating all the activities of a busy family today. (Removing all the work from the kitchen table daily is time-consuming and risky — something always gets lost in the shuffle!)

Some days even a workable plan won't work. No matter how organized a woman is or how well she has managed her time, inevitably there will be times when outside problems bring trouble. Interruptions are never pleasant, and as long as there are chicken pox, cars that go on the blink, and cereal bowls that fall off of tables ... the only thing predictable about homemaking is that it is "unpredictable."

I have my own "3 points and a verse" sermon I preach to myself on days where everything just seems to be in a frenzy. Before I get all "frizzed out," I stop and remind myself:

1. **This won't last forever.** It's hard to convince yourself of that when you've been up every two hours each night with a colicky baby for three weeks straight (or the car has been in the shop three days longer than you planned, or you have just spent four days mopping water in the basement and it's still raining!). Nevertheless, it IS true.

2. **Everybody else has bumpy spots in their road, too.** For many years I thought I was the only one in the world who got bogged down. It appeared to me that everyone else got everything done and was ready for company at the drop of a hat! "Their houses must always look like the covers of *Better Homes and Gardens*," I believed.

WRONG! Besides, I am learning that I would rather have my family enjoy being with me rather than spending my life trying to impress others with my cleaning proficiency.

3. **God cares.** When I finally stop long enough to look at any stressful situation in its proper perspective, I realized what I needed to remember all along. God is with me during the bad times as well as the good. He knows me in my distress and whether or not I get my chores done is not always the most important agenda of the day. Sometimes, to quiet my busy self is far more valuable to my relationship with Him. Often those so-called "interruptions" are promptings to put aside my own pursuits to make time for the Lord.

I Corinthians 10:31 tells me that "Whatsoever ye do , do ALL to the glory of God." Yes, I can even wipe up spilled milk and empty trash for God's glory! That's what Mary and Martha learned the day Jesus came to their home. To serve others is right and noble, but we must jealously guard our time spent alone with God. Overcommitment and physical exhaustion are the sources of many relationship conflicts in the home. With God's guidance, I can control my schedule, rather than letting it control me. When I allow well-intended activity to place demands on me so much that I do not focus on the Lord and His Word, I grow lonely, stagnant, and powerless.

First Things First

In making life-style changes we are seeking a balance that will enhance your quality of life and effectiveness for the Lord. We all know people who have lost their family because work or even Christian service consumed them. Learning to pronounce the simple word with two letters spelled "N-O" is vital to achieving balance. This one is especially hard for me as a pastor's wife! I used to feel like I would hurt someone's feelings if I said I could not do something they asked of me.

But I find I am much less exhausted and more productive in the areas I HAVE chosen to take on, now that I have prioritized what is important in my life.

Our society tends to look on busyness and a frantic life-style with admiration. We often confuse busyness with importance! With this philosophy, it's no wonder that women who are out to earn more and more money or a name for themselves end up living very lonely lives. They find themselves without a social life, no rest and relaxation, and relationships that continually fragment due to imbalances of priorities. They operate for self first and often self-destruct! May we learn the peace that comes from living out a life of deep devotion for our Savior. That means learning to cut some things out of our day.

"Do not store up for yourselves treasures on earth where moth and rust destroy and where thieves break in and steal. But store up for yourselves treasures in heaven where moth and rust do not destroy and where thieves do not break in and steal. For where your treasure is, there your heart will be also" (Matt. 6:19-21).

Barbara Walters once said, "Like most busy people I know, I do three things at once." Then she adds, "Women must balance their time more than men because they don't have wives!" The point is, combine simultaneous activities: read a novel while creaming the hair off your legs, eat lunch while answering correspondence, combine girl talk on the phone with dusting a curio cabinet. Ask yourself, "Is there a way to make this job more enjoyable ... even fun?" You will soon be thinking of creative ways to combine tasks and motivators for yourself.

Complete Tasks by a Set Time

I got to where at one point I was tired of hearing myself say how tired I was all the time! My day and schedule seemed to go on forever and I had very little available time for anyone. Rob used to try to get me to come sit by him on the couch and watch TV. No, I was too busy! Even when I would join him, I was busy ironing or doing some other task, because, after all, I had a lot to do. I found myself trying to outdo him with descriptions of how busy my days were.

By making a concentrated effort to have all my responsibilities completed by 7:00 p.m. (or leave them until tomorrow) we both are less exhausted and more fulfilled. Evenings become "our" time. Even if we go together to an appointment, at least I'm available.

Take a look at all of the roles that you play in a typical day. Mother, wife, boss, housekeeper, cook, nurse, friend, secretary, taxi driver, etc. Can you eliminate or delegate any of these roles? Also, finding a way to do what you do with someone you like is a wonderful motivating factor. I found this concept helpful in my exercise program. It is far more fun to have a walking partner who is at the same speed and distance level as I am. We enjoy talking together as we walk and the company keeps us coming out regularly.

That Someday is Today!

One of the biggest problems people face is following through on what they intend to do. This is not a new problem. The Apostle Paul encouraged the church at Corinth to finish what they had started to do a year ago. "...Let your enthusiasm at the start be equaled by realistic actions to complete the tasks" (2 Cor. 8:10-11). World-class athletes would agree. To them, learning to complete goals is as important as training their bodies for competition. Making a great start does not take nearly the mental, physical, and emotional effort as does crossing the finish line.

Research on peak performers, both in athletics and in business, finds that almost all world-class athletes are visualizers. They see the goal clearly, vividly, relentlessly, over and over again. You can do this in every area of your life. Then, when you get into the situation, it is comfortable and nonthreatening. By looking at each new day with eternal perspectives in view, you and I can address each task with a burning sense of direction. Each small function of the day becomes valuable if it is done according to, "Thy will be done."

You've heard the saying, "If you want something done, give it to a busy person." Busy people are creative, productive people. I have found that to be true when delegating projects in our church Women's Ministries. As the director I find myself often trying to juggle a number of undertakings at the same time until I get wise and hand them over to committee heads. When making up my team of coordinators I look for the most energetic, creative, and yes, usually busiest women in our church. They are women with a drive which empowers them. They know how to prioritize doing first things first. The job gets done!

Start today! Commitment is the significant ingredient that will motivate you to move from the pitfalls that trip you up and impede progress. Instead of procrastinating, begin today to prioritize, plan ahead, and use your plan to press on. Today can be a real turning point as you "Commit your way unto the Lord, trust also in Him, and He WILL bring it to pass" (Psalm 37:5).

With newfound momentum, begin today in the areas that matter most in life to you! Then reward yourself with fifteen minutes daily with something just for YOU!

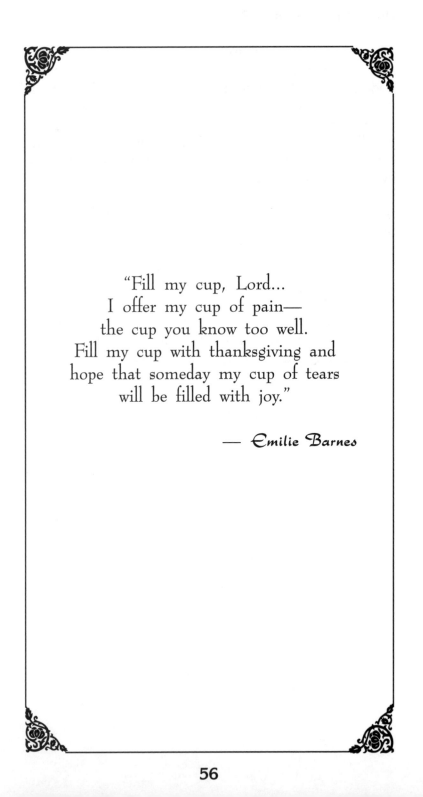

"Fill my cup, Lord...
I offer my cup of pain—
the cup you know too well.
Fill my cup with thanksgiving and
hope that someday my cup of tears
will be filled with joy."

— *Emilie Barnes*

Chapter 4

"The Gift of Losing"
Untie the Ribbons of Your Past

I didn't always feel precious to God. There were days on end when I did not feel like getting out of bed, dressing, and on with my day. I didn't feel like doing the carpooling. Nor did I feel like cooking a meal and doing the dishes.

So, I didn't.

I couldn't pray. I couldn't function. My "bad days" lingered into prolonged periods of feeling hopeless, totally exhausted, prone to feel as if I could not go on any longer.

This wasn't "supposed" to happen to a young pastor's wife. After all, surely I had it "all together." Full of enthusiasm, Rob and I and our two young daughters had just made the move to a new pastorate. As we settled into a new parsonage and community, the busyness helped to shield pain welling up inside my soul.

Once all the boxes were unpacked, our girls had started back to school and Rob was off to his office everyday, I was all alone. We had come from a very challenging, exciting ministry and I had left behind fulfilling relationships and dear friends. With no family nearby and unrealistic expectations, I began to resent bitterly the move we had made.

Healing the Feelings

How could I who was so full of enthusiasm, energy,

idealism and purpose be depressed? Why, that was something that happened to everyone else, not me! So I chose to
"numb out" and go through the motions day after day after
day. It helped cope with the guilt.

With my increasing inability to function or perform, we
began to try everything to "fix" Sharon. Rob scheduled
shopping trips. Conscious efforts by well-meaning friends
attempted to link me up with my new community. It was all
to no avail.

Taking time to examine one's life is the first step of
untying the ribbons of your past to open the gift of losing.
Socrates claimed that "the unexamined life is not worth
living." God's Word also emphasizes the need to "take stock"
of our past, present and future direction. "Ponder the path of
thy feet, and let all thy ways be established" is the admonition of Proverbs 4:26.

So I have pondered. For too long, I allowed heavy
responsibilities to place demands on me so much that I did
not focus on the important, only the immediate. As a result
of all my well-intended activities, I grew lonely, stagnant and
powerless. Meetings, studies, pouring my energies into
busyness did not satisfy my longings. I was still thirsty... still
cotton-mouthed.

It is easy to let this happen when you are the Pastor's wife
of an alive, growing church! "But I thought her cup was
always supposed to be full" is the assumption of wives in
ministry. By slowing down enough to "be still and know,"
God showed me what I needed — that I am human, not
perfect. With that acceptance comes humility before my
Lord, and He alone has satisfied my parched, dry longings.
He has promised, "For I will pour water upon him that is
thirsty, and floods upon the ground" (Isaiah 44:3). Leaning
on Him, not myself... what a wondrous gift!

Don't probe too deeply, but ask yourself these questions
and see if you identify:

- Do I have the "gloomies" day after day,
  week after week?

- Am I having worsened difficulty in thinking, concentration and inactivity?

- Has anger, resentment, real or imagined wrongs, self-pity or guilt been unresolved?

- Am I unable to verbalize my feelings toward those who have hurt, abandoned or rejected me?

- Do I have a change in sleep patterns, perhaps waking early and unable to go back to sleep?

- Is there a change in my appetite, loss of confidence and sense of well being?

I was able to answer yes to all of those questions. So I became a paradox. Here I was in the prime of my life setting out to be a vibrant, helpmate for a young pastor "on his way to change the world." But I wanted no contact with anyone, even my own family; I became a recluse. Physically, emotionally and spiritually, I was a victim of depression.

What concerned me the most was that I could tell everyone else how to get better, but was not able to "snap out of it" at my command. Oh sure, I had offered solutions for years and even counseled many women to find their way out of depression. But when faced with a depleted condition myself, I couldn't remember where to turn.

The losses that I had faced turned inward into anger. With the help of a dear counselor/friend, I was able to finally identify the anger I was feeling. I began to verbalize these feelings in order to break up the emotional log jam. I gradually began to see myself again as a worthwhile person to God, to others and to myself.

The Strength of a Smile

I began to smile again. When was the last time you smiled, really smiled . . . the kind that wells up from down deep inside of you? You are not alone in your suffering. God cares and will not leave you alone. The Lord Jesus not only bore our sins, but also our sorrows and our heartaches.

This present problem that you are facing might be due to your inability to trust God fully in all circumstances of life. Like me, you may be the encourager to all your friends, to all your family, but not be able to react to your own adverse situations. Discouragement blinds our eyes to the mercy of God and makes us perceive only the unfavorable, negative circumstances in our life.

I have never known a woman who has not walked the road of depression at some point in her life. It is tough. It seems impossible when even relatively minor decisions (such as what to order from a restaurant menu) are not easy to make. At times we are overwhelmed by the importance of problems we face and the choices to be made in the process of solving them. Psychology texts or do-it-yourself manuals may offer basic steps to identify problems, but there seems to be only one tried and true process of getting off the depression treadmill.

What does the Bible tell me to do? This is where you determine God's directive. We are healed by His Word in Isaiah 53:4-5. Oh sure, there are well-meaning visitors or friends who write notes of optimism or encouragement, but it is truly the Word of God, the soothing balm of Gilead to our soul, that brings lasting healing and hope. It is there that the recovery process can begin.

As I began to do my part, so did He. One day at a time, one thought at a time, God began to heal my crushed spirit. I had always admired that rugged independent individual who "pulled himself up by the bootstraps." After all, that was the American way! At times, we are all little Frank Sinatras belting out for all to hear, "I did it my way."

Jesus sings another song. His words speak about fullness, of joy, and fruitfulness when we do it "His way." The lyrics of His song include, "apart from me, you can do nothing" (John 15:5).

I had always been prone to think, "apart from God, I can do something." I would admit failures and needs to him, but then I felt sufficient to accomplish many things by myself. It was during these months in the valley of despair that I learned I must keep close to Christ. Each time I have the tendency to take over the controls on my own, God allows storms in my life to remind me how needy I am. We are only asking for trouble when we lead ourselves to believe that we can get along or that we find joy without Christ.

"Replacement Therapy"

Depression. Say it aloud. Even the word itself hisses out of our mouth. Lurking in the shadows around every imaginable corner, it threatens to poison your inner peace and outward poise. Its scare tactics and surprise attacks come when you are the most vulnerable and least expect it. No wonder I fell prey. Making a major move and not knowing how to deal well with the losses involved made our new ministry and community seem neither bright nor cheery. Oh, how I needed encouragement from the Lord! Tell you what — even if you're not in the seat of discouragement at this time, before you and I take off on your next major life changing journey, let's fasten our seat belts, friend! It could get a little rough before we land and a review of the prescription given to me might just do us all a little good.

I like to call it "Replacement Therapy" for women. No, we're not talking hormones here, but the actual replacing of worry, anger, loneliness, fear, jealousy... or any untruth that you are telling yourself. Our thought processes are probably one of Satan's most effective ways to keep us in this form of bondage. I don't need to tell you what lies and untruths you are telling yourself. You already know. But I know the ones that I battle. Perhaps you will identify.

"Replacement Therapy" deals with thoughts that paralyze you. Verbally or in your conscious mind, say "Stop!" Then, by an act of your will, replace those lies with truth, "as he thinketh in his heart, so is he..." (Proverbs 23:7).

Example: When I tell myself, "you can't do that, you're unqualified, weak and inadequate," I stop, then replace that fear with, "He said unto me, my grace is sufficient for thee; for my strength is made perfect in weakness" (2 Cor. 12:9).

Got your pad and pencil out? If not, just stop here long

enough to make a mental list of some of the thoughts that plague you. Here are a few suggestions that will get you started:

- "No one can help me."
- "I was raised in a family beset by worry and problems. I'll never change."
- "God doesn't care about me."
- "The world is too big for Him to care about a worthless person such as I."
- "I've never had any friends. There is no one out there for me. "
- "I can't trust anybody. Everyone I have ever loved has proven that by hurting me."
- "I'll never love again — it hurts too bad."
- "If God made this (referring to self), then I can't trust Him."
- "I cannot help the way I feel."
- "It is necessary for me to be loved and approved by others."
- "I must always be perfect in my achievements in order to be worthwhile."

Challenge these misbeliefs that are stifling your thought life! Replace them with the reality of the promises in God's word. As Jesus has told us, "And ye shall know the truth, and the truth shall make you free" (John 8:32).

Ever wonder why you are not the exciting, radiant woman that God wants you to be? It doesn't come natural for most people. We all have to combat negative thought patterns and the negative emotions that are related to distorted thinking. We can change dysfunctional reactions by discovering our misbeliefs in our thought life. Challenge them! Replace devastating self talk with the truth.

Dr. Frank Minirth and Dr. Paul Meier, noted Christian psychologists, refer to this process as "faith-oriented self-talk." Their research indicates that we talk to ourselves at the rate of approximately 1,300 words per minute. What we believe is partially determined by the programming we absorb from our early childhood, including parents, siblings, peers, teachers, books, TV and so on ... all contribute to our perceptions about the world and ourselves.

If I tell myself, **"I'm just a nothing anyway,"** I can say, "No, I am not," and replace that thought with Jeremiah 18:4, "and the vessel that He made of clay was marred in the hand of the potter; so he made it again another vessel, as it seemed good to the potter to make it."

If I am telling myself, **"nobody loves me, I am all alone,"** I respond with Romans 8:35-39, "...nor anything else in all creation will be able to separate us from the love of God that is in Christ Jesus our Lord."

When negative thoughts want to tell me **"that I can't do it, that I am unable,"** I quote 2 Corinthians 12:9-10, "and He said unto me, my grace is sufficient for thee; for my strength is made perfect in weakness. Most gladly therefore will I rather glory in my infirmities, that the power of Christ may rest upon me. Therefore I take pleasure in infirmities, in reproaches, in necessities, in persecutions, in distresses for Christ's sake: for when I am weak, then am I strong."

When I am hurt and someone has used me, my thoughts say, **"get even."** I replace that thought with Romans 12:19... "vengeance is mine; I will repay, saith the Lord."

When I tell myself, **"I can do whatever I want, this body is mine,"** I am reminded of 1 Corinthians 6:19, "Do you not know that your body is a temple of the Holy Spirit, who is in you, whom you have received from God?"

When I try to convince myself that **"I can continue to sin and get away with it,"** I am convicted by Proverbs 28:13-14, "He that covereth his sins shall not prosper, but whoso confesseth and forsaketh them shall have mercy. Happy is the man that feareth alway, but he that hardeneth his heart shall fall into mischief."

When I tell myself, **"I can't get through this,"** Job's attitude is an inspiration to me. I replace that thought with "though he slay me, yet I will trust in Him..." (Job 13:15).

When I feel overwhelmed and go through deep trials, I replace the thought, **"I'll never make it,"** with "When you go through deep waters and great trouble, I will be with you.

When you go through rivers of difficulty, you will not drown. When you walk through the fire of oppression, you will not be burned up, the flames will not consume you" (Isaiah 43:2 - Living Bible).

When I am afraid and feel unprotected, I replace fear with "The Lord is my light and salvation, whom shall I fear. The Lord is the stronghold of my life, of whom shall I be afraid" (Psalm 27:1).

When I tell myself, you cannot be a good pastor's wife or speak in front of all those people at that women's conference, I replace those thoughts with "Be not afraid of their faces; for I am with thee to deliver thee, saith the Lord" (Jeremiah 1:8).

If I allow needs and material pressures to hinder my security, I replace those thoughts that my needs might not be met with Matthew 6:33, "But seek ye first the kingdom of God and his righteousness, and all these things shall be added unto you."

Strengthen Your Mind or Lose It

The first thing to learn in Replacement Therapy is that we know we can control our thoughts by an act of our will. We can directly command the thinking process that causes our feelings to be negative. Our feelings are only signals of our present self-talk. Feeling bad? Replace negative with positive biblical self-talk. And can anyone speak better to us on the subject of Replacement Therapy than Paul when he said in Philippians, "whatsoever things are true, whatsoever things are honest, whatsoever things are just, whatsoever things are pure, whatsoever things are lovely, whatsoever things are of good report, if there be any virtue and if there be any praise, think on these things" (Philippians 4:8). The result he points out by "thinking on these things" is the peace of God (verse 7) "which passeth all understanding and shall keep your hearts and minds through Christ Jesus."

Peace is the result of Replacement Therapy. Ever felt like you were just losing your mind? God helps you to keep it, "...bringing into captivity every thought" (2 Corinthians 10:5). Talk to yourself in a positive tone. If we constantly criticize ourselves, we will put our entire pattern of living into a depressed state.

Job, Moses, Elijah, David and Jeremiah all showed feelings of emptiness, gloom, loneliness and depression in the Bible. It is no wonder that depression is America's number one health problem today. But you, dear reader, can be in the winner's circle, not the loser's circle. Picture yourself as a dot with a great big circle around you. You are the dot, Jesus Christ is the circle. Nothing, no nothing, can get to that small dot inside the circle without a break in the continuous circle. Nothing can get to you but what God allows. He protects, He secures, and has enabled you to fill your mind with His Word to keep you "in that winner's circle."

Smile! I don't know about you, but that changes me from the inside out. Compare the sparkling radiance of a secure woman with the gloomy expression of depression. Now, who would you rather be around? And what's more, who would you rather be?

What is on the inside comes through on the outside. Replacement Therapy makes you someone very special. Others want to catch what you have found. By putting the emphasis on Scripture and the brighter side of life, you can't help but be radiant! We all know people who enter a room and it seems like a cloud of gloom follows them.

In the same way you exercise for physical fitness, you need to strengthen yourself to be spiritually fit! Exercising spiritually involves time spent in the Word to increase those faith muscles. To achieve the strength and feel "fit," this activity must be done regularly. What are the areas you feel you struggle with the most: fear, depression, discipline, patience, tardiness, arrogance? As I look over that list, it is humbling to admit there are areas I need to make improvement with God's help.

The mere thought of tackling such a list without Christ's help is discouraging. But He promises you and me that if we humble ourselves before the Lord, He will lift us up. Rather than being frustrated and dissatisfied, with His help we can "forget the things which are behind...and press on!" (Philippians 3:14). Look at each day as an opportunity to go ahead, to grow and to change for the better!

"Without even realizing it, our husbands look to us to answer the unspoken question: How am I doing as a man?"

— Barbara Rosberg

Chapter 5

"The Gift of Loving"
Untie the Ribbons of Praise

*A*lthough our Mindy played the part of Elisa Doolittle in the musical "My Fair Lady," I must not have listened closely to the words of Professor Henry Higgins. His exasperation of not being able to turn Elisa into a lady led him to exclaim, "Oh, why can't you be more like a man!"

The obvious answer is: Because she *isn't* a man! Indeed, men and women are different. Very, very different. Have you noticed? Scientists now tell us that men's and women's brains, as well as their bodies, are different. A poor understanding of these differences can lead to conflict and possibly a disastrous future in marriage. Stay with me for this important chapter whether you are married or single.

When following the principles of this "gift" for a loving marriage, you have the potential of changing two lives for the better. One Des Moines wife told me years ago how she diligently "did her homework" each week after our sessions for four weeks. Upon completion, her husband said to her with a weak grin, "I don't know what was taught, honey, but I give you an A+ for the course!" So, from here on out, the seminars have taken on the "A+" title with easy to remember headings:

Accept	Admire
Adapt	Available
Attitude	Atmosphere
Appreciate	

Secrets of an A+ Wife

ACCEPT. Your husband *is* what he *is*. Accept him as that, just as God accepts us as we are. No, we don't deserve it, still God loves us. Such unconditional love is powerful. If you've lost the love for your husband, why not ask Him to help you to restore it?

The first step in the gift of loving is to accept your husband. One lady balked at this idea and said "my husband doesn't deserve to be accepted. He needs to change!" If you desire your marriage to succeed, you must choose to accept him. This will deeply enrich your life as well as his, enabling you both to offer much more to the marriage.

Marriage was never intended to be a reform school. A woman who marries a man with the hope of "correcting his faults" is courting a disastrous future. What was not changed before marriage is likely not to change at all. The Cinderella syndrome where every girl finds a perfect prince IS just a fairy tale! Like everything worth having in life, marriage requires constant work. Far too many marry with unrealistically high expectations, then spend years suffering and complaining.

A good marriage is not based on idealism, but on reality. Respect for one's self and for your partner is essential for fulfillment as a women. By an act of your will, determine today that you will not try to change anything in your husband for one week! Simply make up your mind to do it. When I did, the change I saw was remarkable! My husband spotted the difference immediately! Guess who then began to make changes?

Rob did, of course! When I allowed him the priceless luxury of changing "on his own," he felt my total unqualified acceptance. You may have heard the quip, "the wife who uses good horse sense never turns out to be a nag." None of us women would like to be labeled "nag," yet many of us communicate that message loud and clear.

With loud signs and a rolling of the eyes, we complain, gripe, remind, or play the martyr. Such actions and words make our husbands feel so unaccepted, unloved, unworthy. Your husband can sense when he's not being accepted and is unable to love you as he longs to.

Keeping the lines of acceptance open requires mutual acceptance of the differences between men and women. Keep these common differences in mind...

COMMON DIFFERENCES BETWEEN MEN AND WOMEN

WOMEN	MEN
Tend to deteriorate physically about 2% every 10 years and in our country, tend to live longer.	Tend to deteriorate physically about 10% every 10 years after age 40.
Tend to have about 20% of their body weight as muscle.	Tend to have about 40% of their body weight as muscle.
Tend to be more sensitive to sight and sound.	Tend to favor the left side of the brain where language and logic operate, and to be conquer-oriented.
Tend to be bilateral in their thinking, which means they access both sides of the brain simultaneously.	Tend to be lateral in thinking, which means they tend to favor one side of their brain at a time.
Tend to favor the right side of the brain where feelings, nurturing, relational part of life operates, and to be relationship-motivated and oriented.	Tend to be very competitive and more interested in facts and information and less aware of relational needs.

Accept the Man, not the Plan

Many of us have conditioned our families not to respond unless we repeat and repeat . . . with the volume increasing as we do so. No man longs to be romantic with a "second mother." When he is already low after a day of put-downs at work or failure in an accomplishment, nagging puts him down further. This nonacceptance makes a man clam up quickly. Your husband will not confide in you if he feels a critical spirit or if you are trying to change him.

Life is too short to dwell on another's weaknesses. Try this exercise. Draw a line down the middle of a sheet of paper. On one half, write a list of all your husband's good qualities. On the other side, list faults or irritations. Now, cut the list on your line right down the middle and throw away the faults. Keep the list of good traits with you always. Begin thanking the Lord for them daily . . . you'll find yourself adding more.

Having done that exercise myself, I know what it is like to live on both sides of the fence. Believe me, the grass is greener on the side where I truly accept Rob for the man he is. When I fall back into my old ways, I begin to lead a one-woman crusade to pour Rob into my mold. Boy, does the fire go out in our relationship. Then I try to remember, "My husband is needing my acceptance right now, not my advice." Advising him, or always having a better idea, suggests that I feel he is wrong in a matter . . . and the situation only becomes a "no-win." If he wants or needs my opinion, which he often does, he will ask and I then can give it. If I can't support the plan, I'll at least support the man!

"I Do!" or "Re-Do?"

Admittedly, I am unfortunately a nag by nature. I don't mean to be, it just seems to be an occupational hazard. All day long, I direct people, committees, secretaries, my children when they're not living away, and on and on the list goes. Do you often find yourself in the same role? "Pick up your toys, close the door, take out the garbage, smile at your mother."

No wonder we have to work extra hard at accepting, not advising! I have a special friend who will listen to my innermost feelings. Do you? Mine hears me out and loves me for who I am. I am free to be me. We go on walks for hours and I can just be myself. No criticism. No rejection. No advice. She just listens.

Can you do less for your mate? This concept is from the biblical example in 1 Corinthians 13. True love is powerful... let it overflow. True love is patient, kind, never fails, and demonstrates acceptance. Accept your husband today just as you would a good friend. When you do, all barriers just melt away!

Proverbs tells us that living with a contentious woman is like living with dripping water. You know how annoying that can be. To my surprise, when I decided to quit reminding ("nagging") Rob about the garbage, he took it out the very first night without my assistance. I thought it was going to pile up for weeks! My knight needs to feel at home in his castle, not controlled — that only drives him up the wall . . . or out the door!

ADAPT. One thing is for sure . . . just as nonacceptance brings retreat, nonadapting brings resentment. For years, when Rob would suggest what he thought was a super idea, I frequently responded, "yes, but . . ." Oh, it could have very well been a simple request such as whether to go on a walk or where to park the car, I instinctively countered, "Yes, but . . ." and proceeded to present my idea. In doing so, I poured cold water (or drowned) his idea.

This challenging of Rob's leadership caused him to resent my suggestions and eventually resent me. He began to clam up as a result. When I saw what my bucking Rob's leadership was doing, I determined to respond with an enthusiastic, "Yes, let's!" I about had to pick him up off the floor. It pleased him so much that I genuinely desired to display love by adapting to his plans. By giving up my "right" to have my own way, life became much easier. It shows trust in my man's judgment implicitly. I have found he has never taken advantage of that trust whether it concerns a restaurant decision or which way to exit a highway.

The wise woman builds her home, she does not bulldoze

it down. Proverbs teaches us this, as does I Corinthians 7:3, "Let the husband render unto the wife due benevolence: and *likewise* also the wife unto the husband."

By following this assignment to be a "Yes, let's!" gal, you will find your husband often asking your opinions. He'll begin weighing his decisions much more carefully. Good communication is another added benefit—no cold wars, no barriers.

"Yes, Let's!"

It is disheartening that many wives may look like beauty queens on the outside, yet have no beauty within. *Truly* beautiful women follow in the footsteps of Sarah, the wife of Abraham in the Word of God. I Peter 3:6 tells us if we follow in Sarah's steps, we do well. What makes her such a remarkable mentor to follow?

At first, Sarah did not adapt, or yes, another word would be "submit" to Abraham. It took her many years to get the message that a good marriage largely depends on the wife! At last, she began to adapt and grant Abraham's every wish, even calling him "lord" for respect. That was not his idea, it was hers. For a woman whose name initially meant "contentious and vicious," God honored her by changing her name to mean, "princess." What a gift! And isn't it interesting that, at ninety, she was then given the privilege of giving birth to their son of promise?

The son God gave Abraham and Sarah, Isaac, means "laughter". There was no laughter in their home until Sarah adapted! Her submission and the surrender of her life to her husband is beautiful to the Lord. She truly became a jewel, beautiful and feminine . . . "yes, lets!"

"And in this Corner. . ."

Some women get so mad when they hear principles of adapting to their husband that they do what one woman did in my classes . . . she cried and walked out! After drying her eyes, she told me later, "I didn't come to hear that I should adapt! What about him?" I assured her that we all tend to want our own way and the conflict with ego shouts, "Me, me, me!" Every couple has this problem, especially if their growing up years did not have modeling of biblical submission.

The biblical remedy for marital conflict is shown in Ephesians 5:22, "Wives, submit to your husband's leadership in the same way you submit to the Lord." Now, hear me out . . . don't cry and throw this book out! First of all, you already know, if you are married, that not adapting is not working. Secondly, please note that the Bible does not say that a woman is inferior to her husband, but that she is to be under his leadership.

God has set the ground rules for marriage. There is no way you can improve on His arrangement. When applied, the marriage works because God is, after all, the originator of marriage. It only takes looking at how the divorce statistics have skyrocketed in this century to substantiate that inherent conflict between you and your husband will result when God's rules are not followed. In some states, more couples are getting divorced each day than are getting married!

Strong Divorce Busters

Though equal in status, men and women are different in function. Every organization has a leader and the family is no exception. God ordained the man to be head of the home and the wife the executive vice president. The family system breaks down and turns topsy-turvy in a short time when this biblical headship is not followed. Christ modeled this concept in the way He carried out the headship of the church. This is the plan God intended us to follow in marriage.

Invariably, when the subject of submission comes up when I speak or teach, one or more of the women are like the one I previously mentioned. I don't want to ignore the kind of dysfunction that goes on in some homes when the male uses this biblical admonishment to dominate or abuse his position as the head of the family. On the contrary, true Scriptural instruction is given in the context of mutual submission among two believers. Both partners giving! This is a far cry from the old doormat submission philosophy where a woman has to tiptoe around her husband who does a lot of taking and no giving!

The concept of headship in the New Testament refers to

loving authority, as Christ committed Himself to a loving relationship with the church. Thus, a man is to serve, nurture, provide for, even to the point of laying down his own desires, comfort and yes, his very life!

Now, that sounds like what it takes to make marriage work!

ADMIRE: Dynamic Duo. The greatest need you can meet for your husband is to satisfy his deep longing to be admired. Respect, raises and responsibilities at the office mean little if he is not a hero at home! To women who would like to be treated like a queen, I say . . . treat him like a king!

Amidst the nitty-gritty routines of life, make time to admire your husband. Fill his empty cup to overflowing. And when it overflows, guess who it overflows onto — you!. Have you ever wondered why he doesn't just melt when you tell him you love him? Important three words, yes, but try saying, "I admire you" and see what happens. You have the power to pour into your husband the admiration he needs.

> **Case in point:** Janice's husband threw himself for years into his business, working long hours to fill his inner emptiness. Janice had been critical, expressed complaints even in public, and indulged in murmuring daily. When Janice realized that she had the power to change their marriage, she tried filling his empty cup with compliments. Their marriage began to change. One evening he told her, "Something beautiful is happening here, I can't wait to be with you," and he went on to talk for hours!

A New Address?

You are the one person your husband needs to make him feel special. After all, *you* are the one he chose out of all the others in the world. Admire him when he talks. Look him straight in the eyes to show him you care. Put down your magazine and quit filing your nails! Show him that what he is saying *is* important. Even if you don't care which team won the football game or what the name of the latest truck is, your attention shows him worth and value. Be careful not to interrupt or be preoccupied.

Let him know he is your hero. Never belittle in private or public. I have been in the company of couples where the wife uses verbal assaults to tear down her husband. It is uncomfortable for everyone present, not to mention the squirming, humiliated husband! Pick out his most masculine qualities and begin complementing him today!

Tell your husband you admire his body. If you find that difficult, start by looking for his most admirable characteristics. He may be starving emotionally so start slowly, he might not be able to take too much at once. We listened in class this year as one gal shared, "My husband blossomed right before my eyes! I didn't realize how he had been missing my compliments for the things that first attracted me to him. He claims things between us have improved so much that last night he came and wondered if this was his address!"

Maybe you can't start with four compliments a day (his minimum daily requirement!). But you can start! Your husband yearns to come home hearing how handsome he is, not how many jobs he has yet to do that evening. Your own joy will be renewed, meeting his needs this way. I'm not advocating "using feminine wiles on your husband to get what you want." It is the very nature of love to fulfill another's needs. Admiration works wonders for the whole family. I know of no homes where doses of admiration do not enhance every member of the family. I am not encouraging superficial ego boosts; everyone see through that. Sincere compliments, however, help us all feel secure and confident in life.

I heard from one woman whose husband actually had tears welling up in his eyes as she admired him for the first time in years. She was amazed that such a small gesture could be a major turning point in their marriage. It's often the little things that can turn the tide.

APPRECIATE. We are living in a society where a thankful spirit is often limited to the national holiday in November when turkey is served. What a shame. So many blessings are missed when we fail to appreciate each other and the simple joys of daily life. Appreciation unlocks the door to happiness in marriage. The woman who learns to enjoy common pleasures around her always has a source of joy near at hand.

Sunlight, crisp curtains, fresh bread . . . it's not so much the pleasures themselves that bring joy, but your ability to appreciate them. Gratitude from within is a very appealing quality to a man. Ingratitude is the antithesis of love and loyalty to your husband. He is hurt to the core when an ungrateful spirit is displayed.

An Attitude of Gratitude

One Valentine's day a wife was overhead saying, "Flowers? Well, it's about time!" Translation: "I've deserved this for years. You're long overdue. Another wife reacted by questioning, "What have you been up to? And what's this box of candy . . . you know I'm on a diet."

These husbands were made to feel like a failure. Everything they tried was incapable of fulfilling their wives' desires. So why try? They're afraid they'd only "blow it again." Inside they feel unworthy, like a cheapskate, and utterly frustrated.

Your response when your husband gives you a present is his only reward. How many times have you robbed your husband's joy by complaining about a gift or criticizing this choice? Do you constantly exchange gifts he gives you? Many husbands quit giving gifts early in the relationship because they know their wives can not be satisfied. Why should he keep giving only to be rejected time after time? There's no joy in that!

If you are not exactly overjoyed with a gift your husband gives you, be careful. Express sincere appreciation for his taking time to select it; then thank him for one quality about the gift. The color, its usefulness, or the element of surprise — find something to be appreciative about. He will feel like a king all day!

Childlike appreciation lifts his heart. Have you ever watched how a little girl accepts a gift? She jumps up and down, squeals with delight, and tears into the package! She cannot keep still, and with hugs and kisses she showers her daddy with praise and reassurance that the gift is wonderful! Ladies, let's not ever "mature" so much that we grow out of such expressions of gratitude.

Our husbands need reassurance and appreciation in a society where their masculinity is threatened daily. It is a privilege to carry out the biblical admonition, "it is more blessed to give than to receive" (Acts 20:35). Don't hinder your husband from being blessed!

The Perfect Present

Last Christmas, Michelle's husband searched and searched for the perfect present. Then he told the sales lady, "Just give me one of those prepackaged gift baskets, she always returns everything I give her anyway." He then spent the rest of the afternoon shopping for his two young daughters because, "I love seeing their reactions!"

Michelle related this story at class recently, saying that she now makes a wholehearted effort to appreciate not just gifts at Christmas and birthdays, but groceries, doctor bills, and the very home she lives in. She is sincerely telling her husband "thank you" with her attitudes, actions, and words. Going the second mile has put her husband's tattered ego back together! Any present now is the "perfect present!"

Once we recognize that contentment comes by appreciating what God has given us, we can all be much happier. Marriage can be a barren, dry desert without the nurturing that appreciation gives. Silence is not golden...express your thanks today. Remember: "the heart bone is connected to the mouth bone!"

AVAILABLE. I am highly sensitive to whether or not Rob and I are "connected" both physically and relationally. For me, true intimacy is when two marriage partners are functioning in a nurturing and supportive sharing capacity. When Rob and I are experiencing this closeness, our relationship is extremely satisfying. Unfortunately, that is not always the case.

Make Love, Not War

My marriage, like yours, has its problems from time to time. Last summer, we were about to leave for the church to attend an adult class party. Rob had arrived home this Friday afternoon with a defeated, weariness on his face. I could tell it had been one of "those" days. I tried to be cheery, effervescent, and had been looking forward all day to the evening's social. Nothing was going to dampen my spirits.

I chatted lightly and continued to get ready. Rob acted like I wasn't even in the room and dressed in an icy silence. I was livid. On the way to the party, I sat close to the car door staring out the window. "If only I wasn't teaching that 'A+ Wives' class," I thought resentfully, "I'd tell him a thing or two!"

Putting on our masks of society, we arrived at the church, "Hi, oh, we're fine, how are you?" Each couple seemed just fine as they came in and I wondered my self if they were all in a twit with each other, too. I endured and even enjoyed much of the party, but on the way home, I decided to softly suggest to Rob that we go for a long drive around Saylorville lake with the convertible top down.

"You've had a hurtful, hectic day and the busyness of the week seems to have caught up with both of us." That little remark began to release the pressure for the two of us and we began to talk. Out tumbled all of Rob's thoughts, hurts and concerns. I discovered something important that night under the stars. "A soft answer turneth away wrath..." (Prov. 15:1).

Oh, it would have been easy to drive straight home in silence from the party and not communicate. But a wife; an understanding woman, is available to her husband even when it's humbling or not especially convenient. Give your husband that loving luxury and he'll adore you for it. Your marriage will begin to sizzle — that's a promise.

Two Thumbs Up

There is no greater feeling than knowing you are understood by someone you love. You feel confident, ready to tackle the world with your burdens lifted. We wives, however, have the power to rob our husbands of that confidence when we are not available. They want to crawl in their shell and lock the door. When your husband comes home after one of "those" days, be sensitive to him. He needs your warmth and comfort . . . not discouragement. Crawl behind his eyeballs and see things from his viewpoint.

Remember, he cannot sit down and talk to you if you won't let him. Don't prod or whine; just be available. The first four minutes after he comes home in the evening are critical. They set the tone for the rest of the evening.

Janice found this to be true recently when she made the effort to make those powerful four minutes count. Hearing the garage door opening, she put the baby in the swing, laid down the dish towel, and took the phone off the hook. "My husband couldn't believe it!" she exclaimed. "He really noticed that I was interested in his day. To my disbelief, he talked all through dinner rather than his usual hiding behind the newspaper! After lovemaking later that evening, he shared his feelings the best way he knew how by saying 'this has been a two thumbs up night!' "

What loving availability in action! Be an attitude adjuster by being available in the morning, in the evening, and on the weekends. Thrill your husband by *making* adjustments in your personal and work schedule to be *available*! A truly gifted woman prepares for available moments and it sure pays off!

Sweep Around Your Own Door

You alone must decide how you will live and set some rules that provide guidelines and boundaries. I would like to encourage you to live a life-style that frees you to reach out to others who need the love you have to offer. "Behold how those Christians love one another!" they said in the first century. Stretch out your hearts to others by being available with meaningful chunks of time.

We have lite dinner, lite soft drinks, lite exercise, and, if we're not careful, lite relationships! In looking back, most people wish they had made stronger efforts to improve their availability to their family. My minister-husband has never heard anyone lamenting on their deathbed, "I wish I'd worked at the office longer hours."

Visualize some positive changes you could make that would help you become more available. According to the bureau of labor statistics in 1995, the percentage of women who work outside the home has declined for the first time in forty years. With the enormous responsibilities of working and managing a family, finally women are starting to say, "Enough!" Maybe your life, like thousands of others, would be enhanced and revitalized.

Someone once said that the whole world would be clean . . . if everyone swept around his or her own door. May I paraphrase that by saying: the world would be cleaner if each woman would strengthen her family unit by becoming available to serve the needs of its members. Now, that would be a clean air act!

ATMOSPHERE. Just like no two women are exactly alike, there are no "cookie cutter" marriages. But, one fact is true: marriage partners today are having to work at setting aside time for intimacy. Fast-paced schedules and fatigue have forced many couples into structured and systematic lovemaking, leaving them unfulfilled as boredom sets in.

Sex can restore the spirit and is great comfort to a man. The Proverbs in the Bible speak much of sexual expressions of love. "Man is to be intoxicated continually with the delight and ecstasy of his wife's sexual love" (Prov. 5:19 NIV). Concerning sex, the Scriptures admonish us to enjoy sex regularly and faithfully, if you're married. If you are not, God will give you control or give you a husband!

Music, Mood and Missing Remotes

For super sex tonight, respond eagerly to your husband's advances. Sex, like supper, loses much of its flavor if we offer our husband the "left-overs." But, there is great satisfaction for both partners when the wife is creative, imaginative, and available. Any husband becomes discouraged by negative responses, disinterest and preoccupations. When you do not arrange your day's activities so that you can be available at least the majority of your evenings, one message rings out loud and clear: everyone and everything is more important than your husband.

Stop the nightly treadmill you are on! All of us can plan at least one night this week for intimacy. Lots of husbands would be less preoccupied with work — or with other women — if their wives made their homecomings the most exciting part of their day!

Prepare music, arrange some flowers, take the kids to your mother's, and hide the TV remote! Spray your sheets with sweet fragrance. Prepare his favorite dinner. Eat by candlelight . . . you'll light his candle!

Since the number one killer of love is fatigue, save your energy for your husband. Bubble your troubles away with a wonder-smelling lotion, then prepare yourself mentally to be available to be passionate. A woman's strongest sex organ is her brain and the man's is his eyes. Dress in something lovely so that he won't be able to take his eyes off of you. Throw out that "Grandma Moses" nightgown! Treat yourself (and him) to a new one!

You and your husband will share a precious closeness when he sees that you care enough to prepare for sex to be exciting. What about you, girls? Are you in a marriage rut? Set the atmosphere of availability first thing in the morning by setting the tone for the whole day. Rub his back while he's waking up, give him a kiss on the cheek first thing to greet his day, whisper in his ear that today is going to be a great day. Tell him you wish he could call in late to the office. Make him wish he could.

The foundation for sexual happiness is laid not in technique, but in atmosphere. Marital romance is 20% education and 80% attitude. Knowledge is probably not your problem; the appropriate atmosphere may be!

One of the secrets of loving is to enjoy the moment . . . don't be planning Sunday's dinner menu when the ambiance is warm and loving. Don't break the mood by breaking the news of a dented fender or asking him if he locked the back door. Negative responses and diversions are read as rejection to a man.

Luncheon Special

Whether six months, six years, or even twenty-six years have rolled by, you can bring your marriage back to life! To her surprise, a woman I'll call Marilyn found this to be true after nineteen years of marriage. Both middle-aged, she and Bill had felt dissatisfied, detached, and disillusioned in their relationship for some time.

Desiring to please Bill, and because Marilyn was committed to her man, she tried the suggested "homework" in our "A+Wives" class. Rather than feeling threatened or resentful each Saturday when he would go golfing, she began to learn that her husband needed friends and recreation just as she needed time with her friends.

The next time he golfed with buddies, Marilyn cooed as Bill was leaving, "I'll have a nice dinner and be waiting for you..." She anticipated the worst, but prepared anyway, expecting nothing in return. Whatever happened, Marilyn was determined to love unconditionally, extravagantly, and patiently.

Bill returned unexpectedly early that afternoon; dinner became their lunch; and it was one of the most exciting days of their married life. Marilyn was not searching for anything in return for her effort to give. She unselfishly became an atmosphere adjuster and set the tone for love.

Keep playfulness and surprise alive in your marriage, and discover the romance fires rekindled! Lovemaking is an art you can develop — become a Rembrandt . . . don't let your marriage stay at the paint-by-number stage! And remember, variety is the spice of life. A weekend getaway, one-nighters, or an indoor picnic in front of the fireplace, all work to enhance a loving atmosphere.

Affair-Proof your Heart

Few valuable things in life "just happen." How true that is with marriage! But we all can cultivate and restore our relationships to God's original design. Match your actions with your attitudes to become powerful communicators of love. Just as God forgives and accepts you, do the same with your mate.

We are admonished from the Bible, "To leave and cleave..." (Gen. 2:24). The message here is a commitment worth fighting for! I heard once that good marriage partners are to be C.L.E.V.E.R. having: Commitment, Love, Expression, Vision, Enchantment, and Respect. Pretty good advice!

I believe that every marriage can be a great affair filled with a lifetime of pure pleasure. Yes, it takes work. Daily. But, doesn't anything worth having? Make the commitment to invest in your marriage and develop the "super seven" skills that lead to intimacy. You'll receive dividends that keep on giving! Ordinary marriages can be transformed by God into a full and satisfying relationship for a lifetime! Begin today!

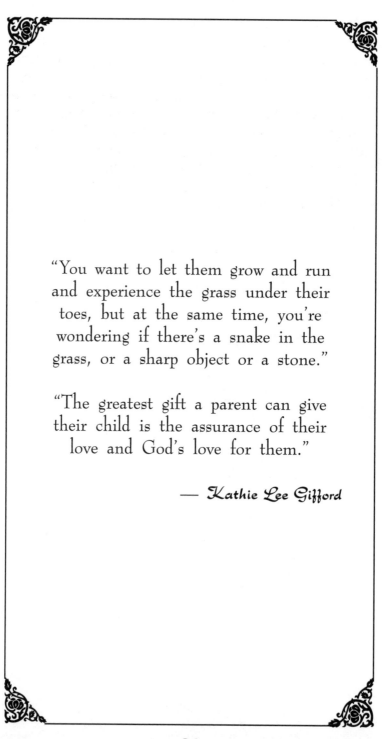

"You want to let them grow and run and experience the grass under their toes, but at the same time, you're wondering if there's a snake in the grass, or a sharp object or a stone."

"The greatest gift a parent can give their child is the assurance of their love and God's love for them."

— *Kathie Lee Gifford*

Chapter 6

"The Gift of Launching"
Untie the Ribbons of Parenting

It is early morning. Literally the first day of spring. Finally! I can see signs of renewal from my office window. Tiny hints of green jut up from alongside our winding walkway out back (we wondered if those tulips would appear!) Perennials throughout our flower gardens are no longer buried beneath brown leaves and the grass is noticeably greener today than it was even a few days ago. Just when I was convinced we were doomed to an eternal winter, God has begun His colorful renewal program!

Oh, Spring, how I've missed you! The drab of our long Iowa winter has dulled my senses and I feel so warmed by today's rays of the sun. Gentle promises of new life are emerging everywhere I look! This is the third year in a row we've gotten to enjoy "our" little Mr. and Mrs. Finch building their nest in my grapevine wreath beside our kitchen sliding glass door. Last year the two new siblings left the nest right on Mother's Day. I cried at the loss, but rejoiced for them as they launched out into new-found freedom.

Terminate This Pregnancy

New life reminds me of my own children. The Bible says, children are a gift, a blessing, a heritage from the Lord, "the fruit of the womb . . . happy is the man who has his quiver full of them!" (Psalm 127:5). Twenty-two years ago, for nine months our "quiver" had been quite full just keeping up with the nursing, diapering, bathing, and all the thrills and spills of first-time parenting. Then, what I'd thought to be the flu turned out to be another little new life beginning to form within me.

After what I assumed to be a fairly routine examination, I was ushered instantly into my physician's office for " a consultation." Emotions inside me began to plummet. While waiting for what seemed an eternity for my doctor's appearance, I strained to read the bold, red scribbling on the chart bearing my name.

I was pleased, even thrilled, to see "positive" marked under the pregnancy test result column. My recent entrance into motherhood had given me joys and a sense of direction I had not previously known. I sat elated, bursting to announce this new-found blessing to Rob and relatives!

My doctor's grim expression upon entering indicated there was reason to worry. He began to explain serious medical concerns. In his mind it was all very simple, "Knowing what you know now, do you wish to continue this pregnancy?" Of course I did not entertain for one moment the thought of not carrying my child to fullterm. This baby's life was not negotiable.

More instructions. Stricter professional "advice." Even pleading. Pictures shown to me of actual babies born with severe abnormalities and deformities from the same condition I was facing. Crushed, I asked for the phone but couldn't dial for the blinding tears. Nurses entered to kindly comfort and call Rob for me. When he arrived, I numbly listened again to the same medical diagnosis repeating that not only was our child's life in danger, but mine as well.

Trusting in Truth

In full agreement, Rob explained that abortion was not an option for us as Christians. It was as simple as that, but simple doesn't always mean easy. There was no such thing as amniocentesis available, though we knew its report would not change our decision.

After signing numerous release papers, we left the office assured only of God's complete sovereignty in the matter. We were matter-of-factly given instructions and told to expect a "natural termination of the pregnancy" within the next 48 hours. If that did not occur we were to call for another appointment at which time the physician would entertain the idea of whether or not to continue treating me until the baby arrived (lawsuits notwithstanding).

I was advised against climbing stairs or lifting our nine-month-old Missy. And so we waited. All we could do was live out our decision through prayer. While the Master Sculptor Himself was shaping a life, I rocked the little child within and sang to her. And prayed.

Not only did God keep our tiny baby safe for those 48 hours, He did the "impossible," medically speaking! Against the odds in all medical textbooks, week after week (I had to agree to be examined every Thursday for the entire pregnancy) our baby lay hidden safely within the cradle of God's protection. I became aware anew of how a mother is the vessel who bears a life by cooperating with God in the making of a child. What a privilege — to be a vessel divinely used by the Master life-giver.

We bore the nine-month ordeal unflinchingly, prayerfully. Rob and I both learned to rest in the promises that God was in charge... not us, not medical science! "For I know the thoughts that I think toward you, saith the Lord, thoughts of peace and not of evil, to give you an expected end" (Jeremiah 29:11).

July 10, 1975: truly a BIRTHday for little Mindy Elaine! I will never forget the astonished expressions on the faces of the medical personnel in attendance of her birthing! Prepared for, yes, even expecting the worst, over and over the nurses and doctors expressed their surprise at her smooth delivery and this perfect little body.

Who do we know deserves the credit for this miracle? The One who fashioned Mindy also guarded her little life safely within the womb and held me in protection as well. I believe that with all my heart. What a gift — the privilege of childbearing! Right from the start, God held the controls of my child's life. I am able to open the gift of launching her out into this world, because before she was loaned to me ... she belonged to God!

You Can Take This Job. . .And Love It!

No job on earth takes more physical, mental, social, emotional and spiritual strength than that of mother. If a woman is looking for the easy life, she need not apply! There is nothing easy about good mothering. It can be heart-wrenching, is tough decision-making, and backbreaking ... and that's just before noon!

When I was a little girl, I used to dream of being a "mommy." The entire image was one of femininity and value. I lived out the dream daily with my dolls by dressing, feeding, bathing and praying with them before bedtime. It was a very real ritual for me (which lasted far longer than most girls in this generation who are ready to "grow up" by age nine — what a shame!).

Ideal motherhood was portrayed on television in my youth by Donna Reed, June Cleaver, and Ozzie and Harriet. They never seemed to tire under the demands and produced "perfect" families. Their children always brushed their teeth, never had runny noses, and followed a regimented family schedule that seemed to flow smoothly without interruptions.

That's not quite how our home could have been sketched in the early days! I did not enjoy the proximity of extended family nearby, where skills and insights could have been passed on from my mother and sister. I thought the right answers for my many questions would just come naturally. I soon learned better.

Thankfully, about the same time I began having babies, Dr. James Dobson began writing books on children and the family. I devoured every one of them. I longed to be a good mother. I know you do, too. Doesn't it deserve our very best and not our leftovers? If you haven't before, won't you today commit yourself to making motherhood your full-time in-vestment during your children's growing-up years? The first six years before he/she begins school are critical!

Motherhood is the greatest cause you can invest your life in. Determine to give your best efforts to what is the most important. That's not to say you have to stay home all the time to be a great mom. Many mothers work at outside jobs. They have to. Today, more moms than ever have to fit part-time work into their schedules just to make the family budget ends meet.

But well-adjusted kids don't just happen. Mothering with a passion shapes lives, attitudes, self-esteem and security in children. What a mother like that lacks in wealth, she can make up for in character and security for her children! I am so thankful for recent statistics that show full-time mothering on the rise for the first time in thirty years! (see Larry Burkett's book, *Women Leaving the Workplace*, Moody Press).

How well I remember teaching for a semester at our local business college when Missy and Mindy were preschool age. There I stood each cold winter morning after morning in the doorway of my child-care provider's home depositing first one blanket-covered sleeping daughter, then the other. Knowing I would not see them until later in the afternoon, I tried to reserve some energy for fun with them, cooking, cleaning etc. But exhaustion was always a major enemy and I never seemed to have time for the "little" things I found so rewarding before starting work.

In between efforts to accomplish everything at home, take time with Rob and the girls, fulfill church and work responsibilities. . .I began to realistically examine whether or not the pressures to balance family and workplace were worth it! I quit after the spring term ended.

Clock Out!

Let me hasten to say, my decision to quit was my decision. I am not including this experience to lay guilt at your feet. Heaven knows, the last thing women need more of is guilt! But I talk with and hear from literally hundreds of women in my seminars yearly who tell me, "the burden of working in the market place full-time is destroying our family."

I am not advocating every mother with preschool age children make the decision to quit her job and stay at home.

I am asking each woman who desires to become a stay-at-home mom, to consider the possibility — it is not impossible, no matter what your financial status! Begin by making some significant changes in your thinking. For too long women have believed society's lie that "mother is a failure unless she dons a power suit and heads for the office each day!"

It didn't take me long to begin considering...personal work-related costs of clothing, child-care expense, additional eating-out or ordering in pizza, transportation, parking and car maintenance, personal fatigue that comes with managing both job and home.

When I resigned my teaching position, it didn't take me long to realize I contributed much more to our family by being at home than by adding dollars to the budget. I had my husband's full support (necessary for this decision or the benefits will not outweigh the "sacrifices").

It is time we get "back to the future" and recapture all those "firsts" young children experience. No two-salary income for "extras" is worth missing that first smile, first steps, first home run! Things will wait, growing-up children won't! They are like wet cement (author Ann Ortland has a wonderful book by that title). Reading books, going to the park, hearing about my girls' day ... these are moments I could have never recaptured! Twenty-three years later, I've never regretted my decision for a moment! I can always go back to work ... I could never recapture helping out with homework projects, attending recitals, tackling piano practices, or catching butterflies for science projects.

It's time this generation says, "Enough is enough!" As good as most day-care centers are, there is no way children can get the same attention as they would from their own mother. I'm thrilled that full-time mothering is back in style! (Marilee Horton's book, *Free to Stay at Home* has many practical suggestions for how a woman can save her family money through being a "working-in-the-home-mom").

Invest in Lives, Reap Huge Dividends

Confident, well-adjusted, loving children come from families in which the mother's role is to provide a high standard of life, not just a high standard of living. It never matters how many rooms a house has, as much as what goes *on* in those rooms! What better antidote for the loneliness and lack of nurturing kids experience today!

"Just a Wife and Mother?"

If you're like me, you regard parenting as one of the toughest and most rewarding jobs on earth. How many times have you seen a woman drop her head and in an apologetic tone of voice say, "Oh, I'm just a wife and mother." That's like being depressed about being just a millionaire or just a queen! There is no position that offers greater fulfillment than to be a wife and mother, or as the Bible terms it, "a keeper at home" (Titus 2:5).

Being a "keeper at home" may require some radical changes in life-style for the whole family. The old adage that "quality time" is better than "quantity time" is simply not true when it comes to building a home. Being an effective wife and mother requires both. There were times when Mindy and Missy would be playing or working on a project in another part of our house, but would peek around a corner to see where I was or what I was doing. "Just wanted to see where you are," they'd say.

Mom is needed to meet the emotional needs of her family, primarily by just being there when they leave and when they come home, and by being available to listen, share, love, and care. She is needed to meet the spiritual needs of her family through time invested in teaching her children the ways of God in everyday, real-life situations. This is particularly important at the time of a hurt, embarrassment or crisis in a young child or teen's life ... not hours later "when mom gets home."

Increased numbers of "latchkey youngsters" and teens coming home to empty homes day after day only increases the chances of promiscuity, rebellion and poor choices of television programming. More than one teenage girl has told me in recent years how that access to an empty house created greater opportunities for sexual activity in her home ... often in the parent's own bedroom. "A child left to himself bringeth his *mother* to shame" (Proverbs 29:15).

Short-Term Pain, Long-Term Gains

Even good parenting, like cars, needs a tune-up now and then. Maybe yours does now! We are not like the lonely Maytag repairman who just sits around all day waiting for someone to need us! We are needed! Needed to persevere at this precious role of mothering, even when the pay back isn't immediate. It pays off in the long haul, please believe me!

I am encouraged presently by my dear friends who are young mothers of preschool or elementary-age children. Through their lives I guess I see a glimpse of myself 20 years ago. Karen, Twila, Connie, Brenda, Kim, Stephanie, Rochelle, Liz, ... I could fill a page of real-life moms' names, who with steel-strong character, are sculpting out lives of character for their children by providing the security that being a keeper at home brings!

Ask any one of them if the choices they have made have been worth it. Ask them if they sacrifice; sure they do. But, I guarantee you, each gal would hasten to add a long list of tremendous rewards and satisfying benefits. They are frugal consignment shop buyers/sellers and garage sale "queens." Each one and their entire family dresses like a fashion plate! They trade-off or barter for baby-sitting, maternity clothes, toys for their appropriate children's ages, and other services such as wallpapering and stenciling. Each also is creative in wisely earning additional resources by selling jewelry, home products, computer typing for businesses, or day care. I am witness to the fact that their households function much more smoothly as a result of these choices!

The encouragement and camaraderie these young mothers share helps them achieve their ultimate goal in life as a mom: seeking to glorify God in the best way possible. No career outside her home could possible give these women greater opportunities to develop and maximize skills as an artist, teacher, manager, efficiency expert, seamstress, economist, nutritionist and a host of others!

The highest fulfillment anyone can ever experience is to be found in meeting the needs of others. So-called sociologist and psychologist "experts" may have chimed in to invite women to become loosed from the "shackles of servitude." Actually, true fulfillment comes as a result of helping and serving others. May God grant to us a fresh outpouring of humility and brokenness so that He can use our lives as instruments of service to others!

It is in serving that we gain, not lose. The heart attitude of a servant is beautifully illustrated in Mary's response when the angel told her she had been chosen to bear the life of the Son of God. Knowing the inconvenience and sacrifice that would be required of her, she humbly answered, "I am the Lord's servant; may it be unto me as you have said." The woman who seeks to be served and who resents serving will tear down her home, not build it up.

Stand Up! Stand Out! Stand Alone!

Returning to the purpose and function for which God created us as women requires standing up for that right in a world that is full of wrong. Standing up might mean swimming against the popular tide today in order that we recapture the ground that has been lost. Ungodly choices made by mothers of recent generations have not equipped young mothers with prudent role modeling. Expect criticism from women who are uncomfortable or who misunderstand the quiet trust within you that guides your decisions.

Out of a heart for God, I am motivated to stand out! No one likes to be known as a "weirdo." We would all rather "fit in," but there are times for standing out in a crowd as a loving expression and testimony for what is right. Morality, purity, honesty, kindness ... these character qualities are fibers that need to be tightly woven into the fabric of our homes. I know personally the empty feeling of standing out while "everybody else is doing it." Being invited with all the other gals, yet turning away because of the appearance of compromise or improprieties involved is not easy.

In her best-seller, *What is a Family?*, Edith Schaeffer devotes her longest chapter to the idea that a family is a "perpetual relay of truth. A place where principles are hammered and honed on the anvil of everyday living."

Then she lists the following principles for us to teach by example:

- **Determination.** "Stick with it, regardless."

- **Honesty.** "Speak and live the truth-always."

- **Responsibility.** "Be dependable, be trustworthy."

- **Thoughtfulness.** "Think of others before yourself."

- **Confidentiality.** "Don't tell secrets. Seal your lips."

- **Punctuality.** "Be on time."

- **Self-Control.** "When under stress, stay calm."

- **Patience.** "Fight irritability. Be willing to wait."

- **Purity.** "Reject anything that lowers your standards."

- **Compassion.** "When another hurts, feel it with him."

- **Diligence.** "Work hard. Tough it out."

Great list! Over the long haul, it *is* possible to develop these qualities in yourself. Then and only then can we teach them and expect them from our children. Your child will become so much more what you are and do than what you say! The key to your child achieving qualities is your mastering them first!

Just when you think you have your kids figured out, brace yourself! Everything from homework to discipline becomes a difficult task when we are not confident we can handle the tough assignment. Anyone can parent, but successfully making it to the finish line requires standing alone! Stay on your child's team, even if it appears to be a losing team. You'll be glad you did!

Standing alone is not a new concept. Anyone who really accomplishes anything in life has to be motivated by this lifelong commitment. For many years, as I have traveled and listened to the hearts of women, I have been grieved to watch the physical, emotional, mental and spiritual devastation suffered by women who have been deceived. Many have paid painful consequences in their consciences, bodies and emotions and in the lives of family members because they did not stand alone. Free sex, abortions, deviant alternative marriages, homosexuality, secular "me-first" life-styles, no-fault divorce etc. have left women angry and defeated. Be willing to stand alone if you promote virtue, modesty, femininity and the Proverbs 31 significant role of women. If our homes are to be graced with children who obey, love, and be all they can be in this world, then we have a responsibility to stand up, stand out, and yes, often we must stand alone! It is my prayer that God will raise up a generation of mothers for the 21st Century who will prove to the world through their lives and influence that God's way works!

Mothers, Give Up!

All of our lives we hear, "Never give up: Run that race as fast as you can." "Keep trying on that diet-you can do it!" "Never, never give up!"

The world cries "liberation" through a life-style of independence. In sharp contrast, however, is the call from God that invites women to find true freedom through a life of loving, serving, obeying, trusting, and humbly giving up their own lives on the behalf of others.

Matthew 23:11: "He that is greatest among you shall be your servant." Even nature itself initiates the principle of giving up. Buds must die and fall so leaves may follow on the tree's branches. A single grain of wheat contains the potential of becoming many. . .but only by dying first.

Instant gratification is deferred and many a mother's dreams "are put on the back burner awhile." Mothers, be willing to give up time reading the latest gardening magazine ... to read Mother Goose with your youngster. Give up loose change set aside for a project of your own so that your eldest can have those track shoes. It would mean so much to him to be a part of "the team." A scratched knee needs to be band-aided at the time of the injury, not when it's "convenient" for our schedule.

Our families are the most discerning audience we will ever have. They know better than anyone else if we "practice what we preach." The little lad in John 6 gave all he had to Jesus. His one sack lunch would have fed one ... when he gave it all away five thousand lives were touched!

A few years after my first book was published, I was asked, "Why have you not written another book?" My answer came quickly, "I am busy writing two ... I've been working on one for nine years, the other for eleven."

"My," my friend replied, "These must be quite awesome pieces of work!"

"Oh, they are!" I exclaimed. "They sure are!" Now that these two "books" are at college and my parenting is long-distance, I have the time to work on my "back burner" projects — some of them have been brewing for years.

Yes, I was taught by my mother's example this essential lesson. I observed all during my childhood, Mother's hopes and dreams were often placed on hold so that my sister, brother, and I could enjoy a safe haven at home. Among the stresses, moves, and changes our family went through, her support was there. This greatly enhanced any undertaking I tried to endeavor and more often than not, Mother's involvement was due to great personal sacrifice on her part.

"Except a corn of wheat fall into the ground and die, it abideth alone; but if it die, it bringeth forth much fruit" (Jn. 12:24).

That is f-a-m-i-l-y.

As I look through the volumes of photo albums our family has filled in twenty-five years, I see the story of our lives together. It doesn't take an astute observer to realize we are a family in every sense of the word. Just four of us, not a large unit, but family nevertheless.

Since before any of us were born, God planned for us to

share our lives with each other. He knew exactly how our strengths and weaknesses would balance one another. He knew the richness of the depth of love we would share, and the understanding of mutual trust would provide hope during the tough times. He knew we would cry together. . .hug, teach, serve, and love together!

Lapsitting — Memory Making

Our picture books show, as I'm sure yours do, memories of everything from births to black eyes. They weave our story of the everyday routine insignificant incidents as well as the "biggies" — the weddings, valuable honors, and moments in the spotlight! Memories sustain us in the tough times. It is impossible to overemphasize their importance. Some of our pictures show one of our favorite memories together — lapsitting. Simple times together just lovin' one another. Sometimes sharing a story. Sometimes tickling. Sometimes just sharing a lap ... the closeness of each other's affection and love.

Just last night, Mindy called from a thousand miles away with "homesickness." It's not as easy to comfort long distance as it was when crawling up on my lap would do. We found great comfort recalling precious memories of last summer. Realizing summer break from her college begins in just six short weeks ("count it by 6 Mondays, it sounds shorter!") helped her to be encouraged.

"Train up a child..." states Proverbs in the Bible. Not only should children have memories of love and comfort, the best place to teach guidelines of right and wrong is in the home. Responsibility and rules develop ownership and a sense of belonging.

Try a Little Shaving Cream

When asked how I have been able to enjoy my children through the teenage years, I've said, "Be consistent with discipline, love, and expectations during the early years. . . you'll sit back and treasure the older years." Yes, it is trying to our souls and takes a lot of training and retraining to raise young children, but the rewards are worth it!

Make it easy for your children to do the right thing ... and hard to do the wrong thing! Design "rules" and responsibilities to be followed strictly ... and don't threaten, scream, and beg for them to be followed! Even the youngest child knows what mom's breaking point is and will not adhere to a request if he is used to her voice pitch going high, then higher, and finally highest! We desperately need designated expectations for our children — in the long run the dividends will be tenfold for you and your child.

We've all heard a frustrated mother in the grocery line scold and threaten, but not carry out her threats. "If you do that one more time, I'll..." Five times later, she's still scolding, but not carrying out her threats. The best policy is to "always enforce the rules." Rob and I found that the clearer the rules were stated (and the fewer), the easier they were to enforce. Ambiguity caused confusion and both we and our girls ended up frustrated and angered if we had not set clear guidelines.

Routines for mealtimes, bedtimes, homework, instrument practices and daily tasks are essential to keep the household running smoothly. There are no "quick fixes" to child-rearing ... it takes a strong commitment to the daily routines and tasks. This is where mothers need strong wills of steel. By an act of our will we choose to provide guidelines and as much routine as possible for our families. Running helter-skelter without the flow of planned-out routine frazzles everyone's nerves, including newborns. Routines firmly fix in our children's minds: This is how we do things. This is where things go. This is what we as a family are all about.

Supper times can provide the gathering time where the family regroups, manners are taught, and family members communicate and coordinate schedules. "But," you wail, "supper time is the most frantic hour of the day!" Try involving the family members in setting the table, filling the glasses etc. Food preparation can be done largely before 4:30 in the afternoon when everything gets crazy! If you make spaghetti sauce, freeze half for another meal. Two meat loaves are just as easy as one — freeze the second!

Have your young child complete homework or create a

card for a grandparent at the counter nearby while you put finishing touches on dinner. Instead of chasing a toddler or letting him play at your feet, keep him busy during dinner preparation with a squirt of shaving cream on the counter or high chair tray. They love finger playing with it. It is a soap so they will taste it only once. You can alternate this activity with whipping cream, clay, toothpaste, play-dough, finger painting, and bread or pie crust dough! They love it!

Dream Forever Dreams

Teaching small children is creating a bit of the future right before your eyes. Remember, they are all different. "Precept upon precept..." means we are to seize the teachable moments! Help children to know how to do what is right. I've never known a child who needed to be taught to lie, steal, cheat...those seem to come naturally.

Be your child's number one motivator! Children who grow up in environments full of put-downs, negativism, or belittling nicknames grow up to be critical adults. Be positive and uplifting. The most powerful form of discipline is praise!

Praise your child in private, one-on-one, and in public: in written word with cards and love notes on her pillow: with little uplifting compliments in his lunch right in-between the sandwich bread!

See your children through eyes of "potential". . .God is not finished with them (or you) yet! Use much grace in your upbringing. Complaining, objecting, criticizing and putting down your child's dreams will wound his spirit until he gives up. After all, if he feels he can't ever please, why keep trying?

I have watched in two actual home situations where the parents turned their child's behavior around for the better by *positive* reinforcement, rather than negative. Dr. James Dobson states, "Verbal reinforcement can be the strongest motivator of human behavior." Consider the tremendous impact of your words and comments.

If you desire your child to be kind, praise her every time kind deeds and words are observed (and say nothing when unkindness is observed). You will be surprised in a very short time how her behavior is modified for the better in the future! I have personally seen countless children change for the better while working in our public school system and families in our churches.

"Caught Being Good"

This world needs committed parents who are willing to spend the effort and necessary time to love our next generation. Don't get discouraged in this all-important task! Just as we used to give the little "I was caught being good!" bear sticker to our kindergartners when they were caught being responsible, I want to affirm you in your job as a mother. Consider yourself recognized and esteemed! Today may have been one of those days you felt "no one cared."

I do! God does! God has given us precious children. They are truly a gift in every sense of the word. He says, "Let the little children come unto me, and forbid them not..." (Mark 10:14).

What does the Bible Tell us About Raising Our Children?

Deuteronomy 6:5-9

1. Do my actions indicate that I truly love the Lord *my* God with all my heart? Should my actions change? How?

2. Is my "parenting style" one that reflects God's plan for raising my children?

3. What are the goals I have for my children? Do they reflect God's plan or mine?

4. What new goals should I have for my children?

5. What do I value most in my life? Should my values change? How?

6. What do my children believe I value most in my life?

7. What specific changes do I believe God would have me make in my life in order to raise my children according to God's plan?

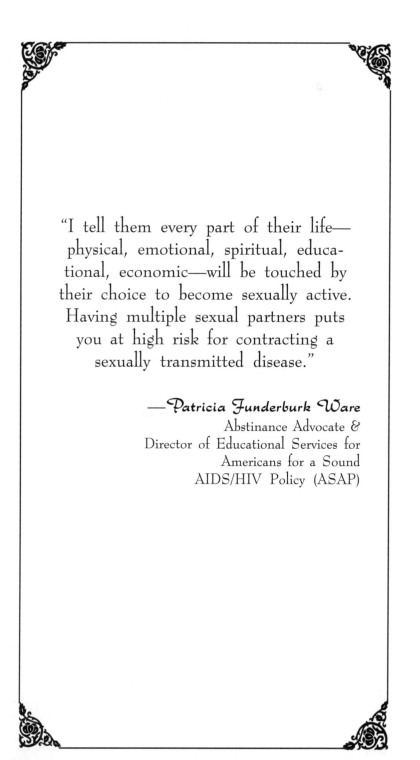

"I tell them every part of their life—physical, emotional, spiritual, educational, economic—will be touched by their choice to become sexually active. Having multiple sexual partners puts you at high risk for contracting a sexually transmitted disease."

—*Patricia Funderburk Ware*
Abstinance Advocate &
Director of Educational Services for
Americans for a Sound
AIDS/HIV Policy (ASAP)

Chapter 7

"The Gift of Longing"
Untie the Ribbons of Purity

Since I've been "duetting" with Rob for twenty-five years, I make it a point to keep in touch with, listen to, and spend a great deal of my time with women who are "soloing." Many of my friends are, for one reason or another, single. Some are soloing by choice; others by circumstances not in their control. Some by divorce and still some by widowhood. There seems to be much I am learning from and sharing with these dear ones.

Whenever I am asked to speak to a group of singles I am usually coached to address the subject of loneliness. Now, I know this is a viable subject of concern for most single women, but I always smile a little on the inside because truthfully, do you know who has the most problems with loneliness? People. All people. Women from all walks of life! In fact, of all the single and married women I meet with — often the loneliest woman is not the one soloing, but the one duetting.

How about you? When's the last time you had to ward off the icy winds of loneliness? Do you know its bitter grip? I believe I do!

Loneliness Became My Friend

During my childhood I had a lot of time to be alone. When

I was just three years old, my birth-mother went home to be with the Lord, leaving two daughters and a young husband/pastor frozen by the sudden loneliness. We know how loneliness can chill to the very marrow of our bones. At such a young age, all the props of security were knocked right out from under me. I was continually in a state of upheaval, being moved around every few months to stay with whatever relative or family in the church could house my sister and I for awhile.

When Suzanne, my sister, entered grade school two years before me, I spent much of my time playing alone. Solitude forced me to invent games that one person could play. I learned to be very creative and imaginative (not *all* that creativity was always appreciated, I might add... with a smile).

I learned to make special times out of silence — times to just listen to the sounds and observe the world around me. I spent countless hours giving "speeches" and telling endless stories from my favorite tree stump (my stage) to imaginary audiences. I acted out every book I would read. My favorite character was to become Laura Ingalls Wilder. What a sight I must have been with a belt wrapped around the handlebars of my bike! Holding on to these "reins" I would ride my "horse" as Laura through the Big Woods, gather berries, then ride back to our home on the prairie!

An even more comical sight must have been my "dog" following behind the bike. By removing the small rubber ball from its paddle (remember those?) then tying the elastic string to my bike, "Rover" followed me everywhere I'd go!

Even after my daddy married my dear godly mother who raised me, our family moved almost every two years until I was thirteen. Making and losing friends, continually changing schools, houses, and churches gave me a very real sense of aloneness.

Today, I am especially thankful for those years of rootlessness and the lessons they forced me to learn. God was giving me just the right background He knew I would need to prepare me for times down the road. Through those years I learned the proper way of coping with the loneliness of being a pastor's

wife, the loneliness of living several states away from extended family, the special loneliness required for hours of
study to speak, travel and write. Loneliness turned out to be
a friend, not a dreaded enemy. Perspective makes all the
difference in the world.

Some women must do everything with an entourage,
turn television or the radio on upon entering a room, and have
to be surrounded with noise or people all the time. I, on the
other hand, am remarkably comfortable with solitude. In His
own unique way God was laying the groundwork throughout
my childhood where I would adjust to, even thrive in the
quiet times. While there is no one who is more of a people-
person than I am; I also cherish times when I can draw away
for awhile. You can too!

Being Alone vs. Being Lonely

Loneliness is different from aloneness.

Recognize the intricate difference between being alone
and being lonely. Everyone can profit from times alone.
Prayer, study, work, exercise ... each brings a heightened
change of tempo and perspective when done alone. During
the days when my schedule is hectic and demands are
especially grilling, even a brief period of alone time is very
welcome. There must be moments in each day that provide
us with occasions to refuel. Seeds that grow to become the
fruits of the Spirit are, more often than not, planted in the soil
of solitude during quiet and private times.

Jesus demonstrated this need when we find Him slipping
away from the mounting pressures of the crowds. He simply
disappeared into solitude. He needed the refueling, rest, and
soothing balm to the soul that only solitude can bring. How
much more do we need it! Jesus implies that it not only is all
right to be alone, but it is an absolute necessity to our
emotional, spiritual and physical health.

Could it be that Christ wants us to discover something
about who we are and what we could become if we free
ourselves from the necessity of always being with other
people? Sometimes the most "spiritual" thing I can do for
myself is take a nap! Get away. Regroup. Rest ... all alone.

Man-Mania!

I do not discount the ache in the hearts of some of you who long for a husband and children of your own. I imagine others reading who might be women whose hearts have been broken by the unfaithfulness of a man. Still others might be widowed or lost the chance to marry in years past.

To truly identify with a single woman is to not get stuck on her singleness. It makes me sad when I hear the cruel remarks of well-intending people who mean no harm, but their judgmental comments inflict pain just the same. Their queries might include, "Who filed first for your divorce? Who walked out on whom? Where are the children living? Is a third party involved?"

It's amazing how compassionate our response is to someone who has just received the dreaded news of cancer ... yet, are we as loving to the heartaches of a newly divorced friend? She doesn't need more guilt heaped upon her nor helpful solutions and remedies. The devastating effects of the loss she's facing are hard enough.

Inquisitive comments are not just directed toward the divorcee. Young women nearing thirty who have no visible dating prospects around the corner get (as one gal told me recently) "so weary of family and friends constantly asking if I'm dating anyone as if that's the only thing that makes me worth something."

Perhaps you have refused to give up the "right" to be married. Maybe you are saying, "It isn't fair that I should be single and all my sisters married with homes of their own!" If these are the thoughts in your heart, you are clinging to *your* rights, not accepting life as it is.

A good friend and choir buddy, Mindy Rutter, recently put it so well in these words:

As a single woman, many times in my life people have pressured me to get married, but God has not led me that way. As a result, I have focused on the concept that there are many examples of singles in the Bible; the first and foremost was Jesus. Paul spoke in I Corinthians 7:34 that those who are unmarried can focus on the things of the Lord. "She may be holy both in body and spirit."

I cannot as a mature, single woman sit at home and simply wait for a man to "save me." I don't believe God desires that for single women. Instead, I try to claim Joshua 1:9 "Be strong and courageous! Do not tremble or be dismayed, for the Lord your God is with you wherever you go." With the Lord's help, I must step out, be strong and courageous, and serve Him now with the talents He has given me.

If God chooses to change my life and bring a Godly man into my life, so be it. Until He shows me differently, I can focus on trusting God and serving Him through my church, job, family and friends.

Assuming that finding Mr. Right is the only thing on every single woman's mind is invalid. Value as a woman is based upon the Person of Jesus Christ, not who she is in relation to a man. Single life, for many, may only be one stage in the journey of womanhood.

If you are single, God may replace your gift of singleness with another gift at any time. The same is true with me. Being married presently, I don't know what tomorrow may bring. The life of faith is to be lived *one day at a time.* The Giver of gifts makes the choice of the gifts; I am to receive them thankfully.

Some of you may be going through a "twenty-two year old panic of receiving your B.A. degree, but not your 'MRS.' degree?" Or maybe your mother is trying to fix you up with every eligible young man she meets? Such concern is something I hear from singles time and time again. Their whole identity begins to be wrapped up in finding a mate!

Singles often look forward to marriage as the day that they will really be a completed person and then they can start living. This kind of thinking prevents the attractive quality that confidence brings. Rather, it sends off messages like, "No one finds me worthy. Poor me. I'm doomed to this miserable life in the status quo." Believe me, no man would be attracted to a woman conveying that negative spirit.

Clearly none of us finds that attractive. Being complete in Christ helps us to live abundantly in the "here and now." Has it dawned on you that if you love Jesus Christ and are honestly trying to follow him, that your being single right now is God's will for you ... *right now?*

In the Holding Pattern

Like all gifts, singleness can be a challenging gift to open. I Corinthians 7 teaches that God gives some the gift of a husband or wife, and to others He gives the gift of being able to stay happily unmarried. The idea that only married people are fully happy is not only untrue, it is unbiblical. Jesus was unmarried. So were many of the New and Old Testament leaders including Timothy, Barnabas, Titus, Philemon, Onesimus, Anna, Ruth and Naomi. Some of these were single for only certain periods of their lives when God had opportunities of service for them that they might have missed out on without the mobility that being single affords.

In 1 Corinthians 7:32-35 Paul affirms the values of single life. Don't misunderstand. Paul is not writing against marriage, but stressing the absolute urgency of making Jesus Christ your greatest love whether you marry or not. His desire for us all is to have us free from all anxiety and distressing cares.

The unmarried woman is free to solely please the Lord, while the married woman is necessarily distracted, if you will, from her devotion to God. And that is natural and right. It is what distinguishes the differences between the two lifestyles of the married and the unmarried.

Have you unwrapped your gift?

You may feel like you're in a holding pattern flying around, trying to find the airport. Get your feet back on the ground by a change in your thinking. A closer glimpse at singlehood reveals unending opportunities awaiting you that are out of the question for those in a marriage. Greater mobility, for starters. As a single you can travel, pick up and go just about whenever and wherever you want (an impractical notion when you marry)! When Rob and I want to do that, it takes a lot of planning and obviously costs us twice as much.

Bloom where you are planted! Take advantage of the time to develop your potential; don't become a couch potato. Use this season of your life to enroll in an interesting class, learn that new skill you've always wanted to learn, or go on a short-term mission trip. Undoubtedly, those opportunities will be put on hold or become difficult when a married partner has to be considered.

I have always thought it incredibly wise of my brother/pastor, Steve, for his insight to get in his years of education and summer mission trips before marriage to his sweetheart, Lisa. There is no magic age to marry! Make the most you can of the here and now. Turn it into the "here and WOW" ...and most of all ...RELAX!

That's what I love to do in doctors' waiting rooms. I don't especially like the waiting, but I can usually count on sitting awhile. I take along stationery to write a letter, use the time to catch up on list-making, or simply relax by reading a no-nonsense magazine article just for fun. By the time my name is called, I discover perhaps a whole hour has gone by while I was caught up in what I was doing! Afterwards, the wait wasn't so bad after all!

What To Do While You're Waiting

Whatever your age or status, don't give in to self-pity like some singles I've known. Nearly two in five American adults are single—that means sixty-six million Americans. The number of single-parent households continues to grow, and according to researcher George Barna, "At some point early in the next century, the majority of America will be single."

But doesn't Proverbs 18:22 say, "He who finds a wife, finds a good thing?" It does. This verse does refer to the value of finding a mate, but the word "find" in Hebrew does not mean "searching for." It means "to discover along the way." It instructs us to first be busy submitting to and serving the Lord. Then, if according to His will, you "discover" He's bringing someone into your life ... *that's a good thing*.

The point here is: Don't go chasing after marriage as a cat

chases a mouse (though you may have every desire to)! Remember, God brought Eve to Adam — neither of them went hunting for a mate! Adam slept through the whole thing! Take a rest from your chasing. When you open your eyes... you, too, may find the someone God has prepared just for you!

What to do while you're waiting? Patiently keep praying daily for whomever the Lord has chosen as the mate for you. Trust that he's out there somewhere and needs your prayerful support even now. God is shaping both of your lives for that day when you shall come together in the precious realization of one another. Continue to better yourself — you will attract a man of like quality.

Never settle for second best or marry on the rebound of a recent divorce, thinking, "This may be my last chance." Love doesn't rush. It is the maturation of friendship; you must be friends before you can be lovers. Set your goals for marriage material high! One of my main considerations when I was dating in college was, "Can I truly be relaxed and comfortable ...be myself?"

I made it a point not to date anyone with whom I would be ashamed or whose reputation, attitudes or character would reflect poorly on my testimony before others. Those inner qualities far outweigh appearance, popularity, financial status, and sex appeal. I'm thrilled to report, however, I did marry someone with all those qualities! The Lord does truly give us "the desires of our heart" (Psalm 37:4).

If the answer to the longing in your heart for a mate seems to be "no," take heart! Instead, God may be answering, "Not yet!" Live content as a single today; by faith keep looking forward to the fulfillment of your dreams and hopes for tomorrow. I heard this precious statement years ago. The author is unknown: "God often comforts us not by changing the circumstances of our lives, but by changing our attitudes toward them." That sure strengthens my faith and I hope it does yours!

What if I Outlive My Husband?

Actually, most women will. Statistics show us that

three-fourths of all married women will indeed experience that dreaded blow that life hands out — that of widowhood. Perhaps the deepest scar of a woman's heart is that of losing one's spouse. The separation creates a deep vacuum after years of harmonious married life. What is the place of the widow in today's world? What are the options open to her?

I have seen some women allow their untimely sorrow to create bitterness and heartache in their lives beyond restoration. Then I've watched others allow God to give them a new assignment in life and fresh opportunities beyond their expectations.

There is no more poignant twentieth century testimony of God's hand upon a young widow's life than Elizabeth Elliot. She has been a personal heroine of mine for as long as I can remember. Her story is told in her book, *Through Gates of Splendor*. After her missionary husband, Jim Elliot, was killed in Ecuador, she returned to minister to the very jungle tribesmen who speared her beloved Jim. Years later Elizabeth lost a second husband, Addison Leitch, when he died with cancer. Now married a third time, she offers golden insights on womanhood as she speaks all over the world. She has written over twenty books and hosts a national radio program. She is truly one of Christendom's most articulate and profound writers.

Elizabeth Elliot allowed God to be her Comfort and use her in ways she never dreamed possible. "For I have accepted God's idea of me..." she says in her book, *Let Me Be A Woman*, "and my whole life is an offering back to Him of all that I am and all that He wants me to be."

God places an invisible wall around the widows. "The Lord will establish the border of the widow." This divine security is available to the widow who, through her own faith and commitment, steps within the boundaries of God's protection. Contentment is hers if she will consecrate herself to the Lord and accept her position in Him (Phil.4:11). For every widow, God is the Kinsman-Redeemer who not only wants to meet her physical needs, but also will restore joy and life to her (Job 29:13).

Widowed young, Ruth placed her confidence in the

providence and faithfulness of the Lord and became herself a widow, God's instrument for redeeming her mother-in-law Naomi from a life of self-pity to a life of joy. Ruth went on to marry Boaz and gave life to Obed, an ancestor of the promised Messiah. Talk about testimony to the providence of God in His care for widows! What a joy comes in the heart of every dear hurting widow when she allows God to restore her with fresh opportunities for Him.

Especially touching examples are found in (Mark 12:41-44); the little humble widow who literally gave all she had to the Lord; (I Kings 17) the unnamed widow of Zarephath who extended hospitality to Elijah; and (Luke 2:36-38) Anna, the dear widow who was continually characterized by the many hours she spent in prayer. How true I have found that to be — there have been no better prayer warriors for our family and our ministry through the years than the dear widows whom I know pray for us daily. I'm so thankful for these dear ones, for their wisdom, and the meaningful time that I know they spend even in prayer for these writings.

May God reward you today, dear widows, young and old, for the angelic touches to all of our lives that you offer! May He refresh you "in due season." God help us who are still blessed with our mates to do what we can in lifting some of the loneliness you might be feeling.

Opening Pandora's Box

Remember, the more bright smiles a woman wears, the more beautiful and vibrant she looks! The Bible says a merry heart does good like a medicine. I know for certain that my attitude on the inside at any given moment determines how I look on the outside.

Conversely, when I set a positive atmosphere early in the morning, things just seem to start so much better ... for the whole family! If my day progresses with lost car keys, mangled homework, and spilled cereal bowls ... I have already *chosen* to fight the irritability and meanness. The circumstances aren't the issue, my attitude of joy is!

When you look at yourself each morning, do you like what you see? If not, change it! King Solomon captured the idea, "As a man (woman) thinketh in his heart, so is he."

How to Measure the Quality of Your Love

Perhaps one of the most perplexing questions that has ever been raised is, "How will I know when I'm in love?" Do skyrockets zoom across the sky? Does a little cupid shoot an arrow into your heart? Will you lose your appetite or become constantly hungry?

For nine months I listened to my boyfriend (future husband) say those precious three words without replying them back to him. I just had to be sure — but how? How was Rob so certain that he loved me? I wanted to be equally as confident, but could not find the formula in books or experienced friends. Rob was so patient while I was sorting out my feelings. He never once tried to pry the phrase out of me.

One Sunday afternoon while we were alone on a picnic, I shocked my own ears by listening to myself say, "Rob, I love you." I had not planned to tell him that day — I just blurted it out. I couldn't stop saying it over and over. That's when I knew I was in love. I had to quit trying to reason out my feelings. I tried to be too logical instead of just letting my heart do the talking.

Now, hold on! Don't become discouraged if you aren't one of the few to whom this section applies appropriately at this time. Read on — you will pleasantly find yourself needing this information, and possibly sooner than you dreamed. These ten checkpoints are valuable to you now, especially if you are presently involved in a serious relationship. The checkpoints are even more beneficial to the gals who have not yet entered into a serious relationship. When that special man comes along, you will have the advantage of being able to check your feelings along as they grow and develop.

TEN QUALITIES OF TRUE LOVE

1. True Love Is Responsive Totally to the Other Partner

When you truly love someone, you will totally accept him just as he is. Many women fall "in love" with a handsome face or great body build instead of the person inside that body. You will come closer to that happy-ever-after ending if you marry a person, not a body.

One starry-eyed couple repeated the marriage vows and anxiously set out for a memorable honeymoon. After arriving at their motel suite, the bride began her bedtime preparations. A very shocked groom sat by watching as she removed the flowing blond wig, curly eyelashes, and restraining girdle. Had this man married the young lady solely for appearance, he was to be extremely disappointed. What would he have left after finding out how "deceived" he had been all during their courtship? We need to have more to offer than a few false pretenses of beauty.

Equally so, your future groom *will* disappoint you in marriage — if you base your "love" on bulging biceps and broad shoulders. You will want to be proud of your man's physical appearance — true. However, his high points must be deeper than the surface. What will you have in a mate in a few years when his physical attractiveness begins deteriorating? His skin will show age wrinkles, those muscles are going to weaken, and that flowing hair you so admire will begin to vanish into thin air!

Ask yourself this important question: "Would there be enough to love if all those physical changes took place?" Could you still look him in the eyes (they may even require glasses) and say, "I love you even more than the day I met you?"

I'm not saying that every good-looking man has no qualities deep on the inside. Nor do I advocate you marrying someone whose appearance you would be ashamed of. But, keep your priorities in the right perspective, putting major emphasis on a man's inner character. Make sure it is one you can respect, honor, and cherish for all time.

2. True Love Shows Esteem and Respect Toward the Partner

This statement reflects not only the person's attitude, but also actions toward the partner in a relationship. This is important throughout the dating period as well as in marriage.

I remember baby-sitting for a family with three girls when I was a teenager. I knew the girls' mother, but had never met the father of the home. But I sure felt like I knew him! Through the little girls' conversation and actions I learned about a man whom I gradually pictured in my mind as being close to perfect. These girls were constantly making their daddy little presents, cooking special goodies for him, and doing their chores readily so their daddy would be proud. "What kind of a superdaddy and husband must this be?" I wondered.

Then one evening I was finally to meet him! I couldn't keep myself from peeking out the front window to watch the three girls excitedly run down the sidewalk as their daddy's car drove into the driveway. What a surprise met my eyes! I had this man's image pictured so differently. A very common, rather short, plain-clothed man stepped out of the car. He huddled all of the girls into his arms at one time, answering their requests for kisses and candy. Just meeting this man on the street, one would not be impressed, but his wife had set these little girls the right example. She had shown them that this man was the king of their home who deserved respect and honor.

Anything that causes one to lose respect for the other person is not real love. True love does not find the partners constantly pawing all over each other. True love does not try to convince you to let things happen that you will regret later. You see, when a man truly loves you, he would not ask you to let him do something that would hurt you. This includes you as a person, your body, and your reputation.

3. True Love Always Wants to Give

Many people enter into marriage thinking, "What's in this for me?" In a relationship where each partner needs to be giving his complete 100 percent, there is no room for such thinking. Instead of saying, "Will this man make me happy all the rest of my life?" you must ask yourself the question, "Can I make this man happy for the rest of my life?"

Marriage nowadays is built so much on giving to self. The woman marries because *she* wants to be in her own home, have her own children, and get away from her parents. Men marry because they feel this is the thing that will make them feel worthwhile and self-sufficient.

When anyone marries for any reason other than to bring joy and fulfillment to the person they love, the marriage already has one foot in the divorce court. How true is the phrase, "Give and it shall be given unto you." The only trouble with most of us is that we want the rewards of giving too soon.

I enjoy sending anonymous cards with thoughts of love or appreciation to people who mean something special to me. Usually these recipients never know that it was I who sent them, but I know their day was brightened because of a little expression of thoughtfulness. That's my reward!

This is the way giving in marriage needs to be. The other person's desires must come before your own. Sometimes this means great sacrifices. It may require you to rearrange your entire schedule for some spur of the moment whim that your husband dreams up. It means smiling when he spends the entire paycheck on something for the house when you had counted on buying a beautiful new winter coat.

4. True Love Embraces a Willingness to Accept Responsibility

Many folks say that during the next generation the institution of marriage is going to dissolve and become obsolete. I cannot believe such predictions in light of biblical principles. God ordained marriage, and as long as there are couples in love who also love God, there will be marriages. God knew this was the best way for man and woman to live together. Instead, mankind has to try his own methods to see if they work better than God's. We all know this is impossible.

Some couples enter marriage thinking, "Well, if this doesn't work out, then we can always get a divorce." What a sad thought to be thinking as you walk down the aisle! Anyone who has ever experienced a divorce in the immediate family knows that it is not just a simple signing of a document. So many innocent lives are affected as the pain lags on indefinitely.

When you repeat the vow "I do," you are, in effect, saying, "I will stick it out." Sometimes the going gets rough as making a truly great marriage takes a lot of work. Everything in marriage does not come readily, so keep in mind that it will take your 100 percent effort. When the going gets rough, remember Isaiah 43:2. In this precious verse God promises to be with us as we go through deep waters of difficulty and great trouble. This is why so many marriages fail. The couple forgets to turn to the Source of answers to all their problems. They read sex manuals and see marriage counselors, but fail to go to God's Word. No couple will ever feel like giving up after they have prayed together. While getting up off their knees, they will know their marriage has hope because God will help them.

Divorce has become too easy to obtain in our country. Don't let yourself be guilty of thinking that your marriage could ever end in divorce. If you even entertain such thoughts, then divorce will always be a possibility for cop-out in the back of your mind. Every time some little conflict arises you will begin to think, "Maybe we weren't meant for each other after all." Ask God to remove such thoughts — even now as you pray toward your eventual marriage responsibilities.

5. True Love Is Marked With Joy in the Partner's Presence and Pain on His Or Her Absence

Throughout the year at college that Rob and I first began dating, we cherished every opportunity to see each other. Classes, clubs, cheerleading, jobs and all the other campus activities made those times few and far between. I remember just living for those moments we would be able to spend together. When we were apart I would daydream about Rob and doodle his name all over class notes. I spent much of my time staring out of my dorm window in hopes of catching a glimpse of him across the campus.

Even now when Rob has to go to out-of-town engagements, I enjoy my alone time, but miss him a lot.

This exemplifies a characteristic of love. Not that when your man is away, you will worry continually about his actions or his feelings — not that kind of pain when he's not there. I have enough confidence in our love to know that if Rob were called away for two years of service, that when he returned to me, our love would be stronger than the day he departed. The feeling of pain is due to the loss of companionship and security that his being there offers.

Genuine love is always characterized by the good time couples have while together, and the longing for the partner during separation. Do you enjoy having your loved one around — doing nothing special — just being together? Or are you rather relieved when he's gone so you can let down and be yourself for a while? Consider both of these attitudes when deciding if his presence brings joy and his absence brings pain.

6. True Love Finds Enjoyment Without the Need of Physical Expression

When a couple is sincerely in love they will find moments of pure happiness just by being with each other. Have you ever been on a date when you felt uncomfortable, unless either you or he were constantly talking? You had to keep one step ahead of him so that the conversation would not lag and silence prevail. In marriage, you and your mate would wear yourselves out physically and emotionally if you had to constantly keep up that pace. There will be many evenings when you both, after an exhausting day, simply feel like relaxing together watching television. Have you ever taken notice of elderly folks as they sit together, perhaps in a porch swing or rocking chairs? How peaceful and content they seem to be — just to know that their loved ones are nearby!

I guess this thought hit me as Rob and I drove to our secluded honeymoon cottage. It was located on a lake, a two-hour drive from our wedding location. After all the hustle and bustle of a big church wedding and reception, we were both in need of the two-hour getaway drive. Driving along, I felt my body relax after the hectic year of preparation for that eventful day. A mutual understanding of our feeling was communicated between the two of us as we traveled together in complete silence. I remember thinking, "I never knew we could be so content with each other."

A woman who has to have her loved one pawing all over her every minute she's with him had better check her motives for dating him. You should not feel insecure if he doesn't constantly have his arm around you, or isn't always holding your hand. This is one sure way of telling if your relationship is mostly physical. Perhaps you should consider this possibility if he needs to constantly have some form of physical contact.

Many women actually like loved ones to cuddle them in front of people. This kind of woman feels that the display is showing others how much her man really likes her. She wants her man to always be at her side, never allowing him to have a good time with others. Such possessiveness drives away men instead of making them more attached. A man can show his affection for you by his manners, courtesy and politeness toward you rather than constant physical attachment. The message will come through as he shows respect for you, instead of using your body as a play toy.

7. True Love has a Protective Attitude

The female bear is a relatively calm animal, but let something threaten her cub's safety and she becomes a ferocious savage beast. A human being has the same protective instincts for the one he loves. If humanly possible, a mate will prevent any harm from coming to his or her partner.

Nothing is more discouraging than to hear something untasteful or critical being spoken about the one you love. Not only will this hurt you, but it will also make the protective instinct swell up inside you. You will want to stand up for the loved one who is being torn down. You should be able to trust the one who loves you to do the same. He should want to rush to your rescue when trouble threatens.

I'm thankful that I have this assurance in my husband. I recall one incident where I really was in the wrong, but Rob stood by me and supported my actions. Then later, as we discussed the situation, I realized that I was wrong — and Rob knew it all the time. Yet, he was not critical in front of anyone which would have caused me embarrassment.

Not only should the one you love shield you from the criticism of others, he needs to bring up his pet peeves only in private. Just as a child is ashamed to receive correction in front of his friends, we must not voice faults of our loved ones in public. Your man should praise and exalt you in front of others — not tear you down. If he feels you acted too giddy at a party, he should bring up the subject after you are away from the crowd. When he notices your slip showing, it would be appropriate to draw you aside to inform you of the problem — not right in front of everyone. Someone who truly loves a person will not make a spectacle of that person. He will, rather, talk about her best qualities and bring up the good points.

Criticisms can wear away at a relationship faster than anything else. Sarcastic remarks, even if they start out to be funny, will hurt in an unforgettable manner. Don't get into the habit of picking at the little things about the one you love. Pretty soon you will be concentrating so much on those petty faults that you won't be able to see any good shining through.

It is true that "a friend in need is a friend indeed." This is how it is in true love — each will shield and protect the other. Such assurance in a relationship brings security and knowledge that you will never stand alone.

8. True Love has the Feeling of Belonging

Have you ever found yourself at a gathering and, even though you knew the people there, you still felt very "out of it?" I sure have — and it isn't a very comfortable feeling at all.

When you are in love, however, those feelings of insecurity will change into a deep sense of belonging. It will not matter where you are, who you are with, alone or in a crowd — the confidence that accompanies true love will comfort you. Your love doesn't even have to be right at your side for this peaceful assurance to accompany you — just the deep-down knowledge of his love is enough.

I remember the first week after Rob presented me with my engagement ring. Finally, our love was announced and public for the world to know! I just could not stop staring at that beautiful diamond! It seemed as though if I were to take my eyes off it, it might vanish from my finger. The reason I (and every other newly engaged woman) could not stop looking at that engagement ring was not only because of its delicate beauty, rather, it was because of its meaning and what the symbol stands for. The significance of the ring symbolizes a unified love between two people. Every time I viewed my ring, I was reminded of the love that Rob and I shared. This gave me a sense of belonging and security that I had never before experienced.

It doesn't take the viewing of a ring, necklace, or picture to know such security. When true love abounds, the feeling is automatic. It will just be there — no one can describe it or define it. But, when it comes, *you will know.*

Both partners have to fulfill the other's needs equally. When one slacks off, he himself will suffer in the long run. This truth was clearly presented in the discussion about "filling his cup." When we women fail to compliment and admire our men enough, we suffer by not receiving any overflow from them in return.

9. True Love Is Based on the Common Grounds of Understanding

What was it that first attracted you to your one special man? Was it his appearance, his voice, his manners? Thinking back, I'm sure you recall something unique about that special man that caught your attention and turned your eyes in his direction. When you began dating, you surely found more about him that pleased you. The dating period is a time to discover interests that both partners have in common.

Couples that really hope to make a go of their relationship must have more in common than both liking to eat pizza. After all, how much conversation can be built around the subject of sausage or pepperoni? Plus, a person can only eat pizza so long! I realize that this is extreme, but when it comes right down to it, it's a shame that many couples have just about that much in common.

Not only are common grounds of interest important, agreement on important convictions is also essential. Religious and moral convictions need to be discussed and the standards set   before marriage. There have been many couples who honestly loved one another — but have split up. They just could not cope with conflicting convictions. Had these been decided before marriage, the suffering would not have had to take place.

Being agreed on common grounds early in a relationship will save a lot of heartache when it comes to raising a family, too. Children must not see conflicts between their parents or they will become confused and insecure. This is especially important when it comes to disciplining the children. If children know one parent is more apt to give in, they will always go to that one and become resentful toward the stern parent.

The key to having common grounds of understanding in your relationship with your future husband is for you to set your standards early; then settle only for the man who is equally convicted. If you compromise because you want a man so badly, regrets and conflicts are bound to appear later. True love is in agreement; true love is not based on confusion and conflict.

10. True Love Looks to Christ for Help and Growth

Love that remains strong enough for a lasting marriage can only come from above. It is only fitting, then that couples go to Jesus Christ when problems arise. By doing this, they will grow spiritually together.

Everyone needs to be faithful in having regular, individual, personal Bible study and prayer. In addition — as often as possible — the family needs to gather around God's Word. Even if it is only you and your husband, this precious time of sweet communion can stabilize your marriage as nothing else can. A relationship is not going to continue at one rate. The love will either grow stronger or get weaker. To help your marriage get off to a good start, this pattern of having devotions together needs to be set early while dating.

The trials that come along the way will not hit nearly so hard if the couple is accustomed to praying together. When trouble does arise, it will be the most natural thing in the world for them to go to the Lord in prayer. After all, God gave us this love in the first place. The least we can do in return is turn it back over to Him to be used for His honor and glory!

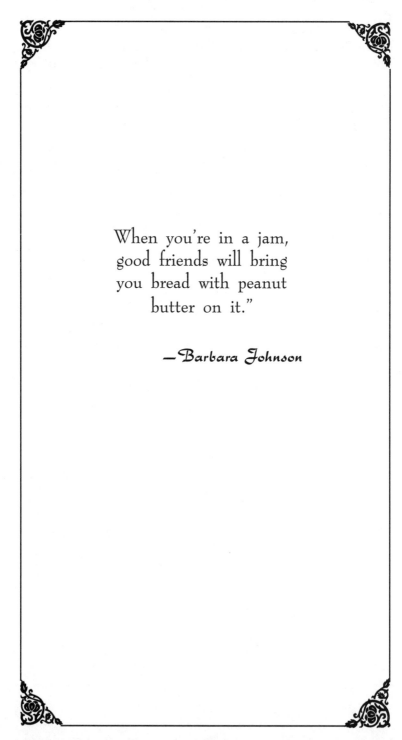

When you're in a jam,
good friends will bring
you bread with peanut
butter on it."

—Barbara Johnson

Chapter 8

"The Gift of Lifelong Friends"
Untie the Ribbons of Promise

It hit me the other day while I was selecting pictures for our 25th anniversary celebration. The photographer did a great job of capturing candid moments from the ceremony to our reception and of us leaving in a flurry of rice. One of my favorite snapshots shows my friends diving for the wedding bouquet. Among them are a couple of friends whom I kept in touch with for several years after college. Then we sort of drifted apart, out of contact with each other.

No, we didn't quarrel. There was no "incident" or animosity. I can't put my finger on it. Somewhere along the line, we just lost touch. Gradually we just stopped writing or calling and quit making the effort to get together. The friendships fizzled.

With a Little Help From My Friends

What keeps you close to your friends? What tears you apart? Women long for deep levels of intimacy in caring and sharing with other women. Yet all friendships have valleys and peaks. It is impossible for our friendships to stay exactly the same through years of changes in our lives. I've discovered firsthand how friendships are altered or even dissolved after a cross-country move, marriage, or another life passage.

When we moved from Texas to the Midwest, I knew

125

precisely which of my friendships would last. There was not enough cement to hold some of the relationships together long distance. My enduring friendships have been the ones that are based on meaningful, mutual commitment. Preserving those special bonds has taken work, and it has been worth it!

Except for my sister and mother, I feel closer to some of my long-distance friends than any women on earth. They listen and give uncritical support when I need it. Now two states away, Carolyn is such a friend ... has been since we were roommates in college. Since I am not *her* pastor's wife, ours is a relaxed, transparent, non-judgmental friendship. She fills a relational deficiency need I would have without her! And what a prayer warrior she is for me!

Women Need Women

Women are "right brainers," or so we've been told. The right side of the brain perceives emotions. Therefore, women are better at getting in touch with feelings. In a world that often encourages women to be more like men, that is important. We are simply more gifted in the "emotional" hemisphere. Our great capacity for empathy and understanding is evidence that the right side of the brain helps in the expression of feeling.

Neurologist Elliot Ross of the University of Texas discovered that "damage to a particular region of the right hemisphere impairs our ability to express or interpret what we feel." As women, we empathize. We affectionately nod and raise our eyebrows signifying: tell me more. Men are more apt to respond with a grunt, an "uh-huh," or present a one-two-three step solution to the problem. No wonder women often call another woman when they just need someone to listen!

You don't find card companies developing lines of friendship cards targeted at men. That would be a financial disaster because men simply wouldn't buy them. About as comfortable as some men get with male expressed intimacy is the "I love you, man!" phrase. Men tend to like to do things together, more at the head level than at the heart level.

After making a move to our city from a southern state, my new friend Barb lamented, "I just need a woman friend, I need someone to understand." I understand that. Each time we have moved, I have been restless until I have found a kindred spirit.

Anne spoke of "her Diana" in *Anne of Green Gables*. "I've dreamed of meeting her all my life — an intimate friend, you know, a really kindred spirit to whom I can confide my innermost soul."

The unfailing love between Naomi and Ruth in the Bible expresses how they were soul mates as well. "Entreat me not to leave thee, or return from following after thee; for whither thou goest, I will go; and where thou lodgest, I will lodge; thy people shall be my people, and thy God my God. Where thou diest, will I die, and there will I be buried; the Lord do so to me, and more also, if ought but death part thee and me" (Ruth 1:16-17). How fitting that the very name Ruth means "a woman friend!"

I can't count the number of times my heart was refreshed by the loving friendship of my mother-in-law. Though she has been with the Lord for three years now, her unconditional acceptance at our very first meeting (hard for mothers-in-law to do when another woman captures her son's heart) set the tone for a deep love we shared for twenty-four years. I distinctly remember it was Mom who initiated the non-threatening spirit. Her amazingly courageous, final good-byes bestowed a heritage upon me that remains central in every friendship I have been privileged to share since.

Sometimes those in leadership think they cannot have any close friends. From personal experience as a pastor's wife, let me tell you that is a mistake. Of course you must use wisdom and discretion, but everyone needs close friends. It gets lonely on a pedestal! Cultivating intimate friendships is well worth the risks!

The ABC's of Friendships

How would you complete the sentence, "A friend is ...?" While God is my best friend to whom I pour out my heart, I'm so glad He fills my life with friends with skin on. Like stars that enamel the sky, friends provide arms to hug, lips to encourage, and eyes to cry with me. As individual body parts make up the whole person, without friends to fill each unique role I would not thrive.

There is a simple secret to making friends. Some advice I heard a long time ago has worked for me in 25 years of dealing with people, largely in church work where I have had to meet and know hundreds of people. The advice was: "people are more important than things." I've summed up that statement in the following ABC's. They can help you learn to be a warmer, more lovable person with deeper friendships.

"A": Accept Other People's Differences.

Just like no two snowflakes or fingerprints are alike, many of my friends and I are very different in many aspects. In spite of all these contrasts, *we do not allow our differences to become barriers to our friendships.* By accepting and taking the time to understand our differences, we can find out we do have some things in common.

Finding out what makes another person tick opens the door to untapped sources of friendship. It starts by recognizing the principle of time. It really does take an investment of quality time on a regular basis to make a friend. That requires sacrifice, loss of privacy, and being vulnerable enough to open yourself up to pain and loss. Friends may move, die or abandon you, but the consequences of living without friends is far worse than the pain of loving.

Few things in life "just happen." I have failed at relationships before because I did not put forth the effort to see beyond differences in myself and another person of a different generation, race, or background. When I have succeeded I have found one of life's happiest luxuries — a new friend!

Some people go through life estranged from a family member and constantly change jobs (or mates) because they cannot accept the differences in others. Could it be that they try to clone everyone to be like themselves? Do they view people as objects to change or fix? Will every friendship weather misunderstandings and trying times? Hardly. I find it very freeing in my friendships when each others' uniqueness is acknowledged and respected, not questioned or threatened.

"B": Believe In People.

People who get ahead in life know that others like to be around affirming, encouraging people. That's your secret weapon to making friends! Start believing in people. Instead of telling co-workers how poorly they are doing in the office, do something to gain their affection. *Find something you like about them.* Say it with enthusiasm. Don't criticize, nag or belittle.

Do the same with your spouse, neighbors, pastor, your children ... the list is endless. Every person you meet is a potential friend. Open yourself up to others — cultivate an atmosphere for a rich harvest of new friends. Meet them and then be prepared to be surprised by the joy that believing in people will bring. Others will want to be around someone who brings out the best in them.

Little girls know this art. They walk hand in hand to school; they hold each other tight and tell each other, "You're my best friend. I love you." This enormous, transparent belief in one another is powerful in any relationship. It affects behavior toward establishing relationships in families, marriages, and the work place. Psychology books often advocate that you assert yourself, do your own thing, taking advantage of others before they can take advantage of you. I've noticed that the happiest people in life I know are the ones *not* pushing and shoving. They are confident in themselves enough to accept the differences in others. Thus, they don't need to intimidate everyone around them to change. I really enjoy being around folks like that. They motivate me to do and be my best!

"C": Cultivate the Art of Listening.

Phenomenal strides towards making a friend and being a friend are often made by just being there to listen. Listening has been called an uncommon personal skill that must be practiced, developed and nurtured. It has also been referred to as the most difficult thing for most of us to do!

Often all a person needs or wants at a moment of pain is someone to be there and care. Sometimes I ask people who complain they are lonely, "Why do you think you are lonely?" They usually answer that they have too many flaws, no one would want them to be their friend, they are afraid of what people might expect of them and they would not measure up. True, friendships are reciprocal, but one person must be willing to take the initiative. Friendships are cultivated by listening. The listener conveys an unspoken message that says, "I value you ... I need you."

According to communication experts, eye contact is one of the surest indications to know if someone is really listening. It is an insult if you are doodling on a piece of paper, looking out the window, or thumbing through a book while someone is trying to share their heart with you. Listening is a valuable commodity that needs to be woven into the very fabric of each relationship.

Show people you care by looking at them — squarely in the eye. Hang onto their words and listen. Shut out all other interests and distractions and let your friend know she is the most important person in the world for that space in time.

Talking out a problem out loud helps others to become clear on an issue. They usually don't need our advice or opinions. More often than not, they just want to talk and arrive at their own decision. Patients spend thousands of dollars yearly in psychiatric offices just to have someone genuinely listen to what they are saying. An hour of undivided attention would do many of our friends a world of good! That's a gift we all can give!

Do you constantly relish opportunities to promote your own virtues? Do most of your conversations begin with, "I...?" I'm going to ask you to step out of your past habits and to think of others and not yourself. When you find yourself more concerned in any relationship with what you can give more than what you might receive, you will discover that you are in a most blessed position.

It is enough to smile and listen. There is little need to rely on nonstop conversation in making friends. You will be pleasantly surprised. Just being there for others — it will change your life. When was the last time you made it a point to be a giver and not a taker? I challenge us all, to begin opening our ears a little wider and closing our mouths a little tighter.

Jesus Christ was a master conversationalist — he listened attentively ... to the leper, the woman at the well, politicians, mothers, religious zealots, invalids, lawyers and fishermen. He wanted to hear what they had to say. That is the only way He could know them fully. "To listen attentively to another is to pay the highest compliment. You are showing that you value what the person is thinking," states Alan Loy McGinnis in his super book, *The Friendship Factor*.

"The Titus Touch"

While Rob is my closest, choicest, best friend, it would be unfair for either one of us to expect the other to fulfill all of our needs for friendship. We both make a conscious effort to nurture healthy friendships and encourage each other to make close same-sex friends since much of life is lived outside the home. I am thankful for and do not feel in competition with Rob's close friends with whom he golfs, lunches, or whatever "guy thing" is on the agenda.

Many men appear afraid to build close relationships with the same sex in our homosexuality-sensitive society. They are running scared from building deep man-to-man relationships because of that stigma. What a shame! I'm glad to see more interest stirring in our church men's ministry. Soul mates, mentors, and just good old fashioned clean fun for a man are hard to come by in the dog-eat-dog business world (you don't have to have a bosom to have a buddy!).

Ladies, let's not forget to encourage our men to establish warm relationships with "the guys." A good biblical example is the tender, caring relationship between Jonathan and David. Their loyalty and commitment to one another went to the remarkable level where each was willing to die for the other!

How many individuals do you know who would die for you? I've asked myself that question and found a few. Over the years a few relationships have deepened to that level.

Christ talks of a sustaining love that He had with His twelve disciples. He says, "Greater love has no man than this, that a man lay down his life for his friends" (John 15:13).

We also find Titus comforting the great missionary Paul in the second book of Corinthians. Paul needed encouragement. He was under great tribulation, exhausted, fearful, and "troubled on every side." Nevertheless, God comforted him through the coming of Titus, his friend in the ministry. Paul was able to rejoice and find strength to go on.

Traveling across America many times a year speaking to women has given me a real heart for those dear ones with the "Titus touch." A sweet word of encouragement ... fruit basket or flowers in my room ... hugs and prayers before I speak ... all gestures of compassion and love that display the spirit of unselfish friendship. They mean so much!

Many times we get so caught up in our own little worlds that we are oblivious to those around us who are hurting or who might need attention from someone who cares. Questions to ponder: who are you passing every day that needs your friendship? Have you become too busy to see them?

"Sir, I have no man to put me in the pool" (John 5:1-9). Here was a man trying to do what Jesus asked Him to do, but had no friend to assist him. Not one person took the time to even notice he needed help. Oh, but Jesus did. He went where people were hurting and He reached out to them.

Jesus saw this man. (vs. 6) He spoke to him. (vs.8) Then Jesus met the need of that man. Who are we avoiding to "see" and "speak to?" Every time you reach out and touch someone you make a difference in their life. People are not objects. They are opportunities to show the love of Christ.

Love is Something You Do

There are two kinds of friends in the world. You are one or the other; people can tell the moment you walk into a room. Your attitude either says "Here I am" or "There you are."

Which kind of friend are you? Your warmth, your smile will draw people in to you. A touch on the shoulder or hand silently opens lines of communication. "There you are," you say to others, "God loves you and so do I." The first century

Christians were known by the love they showed to each other. We can catch the world's attention the same way — by loving one another. What a delightful study it is to look up all the "one another" commands in Scripture. This phrase is used about 100 times in the New Testament. The most frequently repeated one is "Love one another," which Jesus emphasized over and over again.

Reach out today — begin practicing God's "one another" plan. In God's arithmetic, joys shared are doubled; burdens shared are halved. Life is too short to go it alone — we need each another.

Some "one anothers" to get you started include:

Love one another	John 15:17
Prefer one another	Rom. 12:10
Receive one another	Rom. 15:7
Admonish one another	Rom. 15:14
Not provoke one another	Gal. 5:2
Not envy one another	Gal. 5:26
Forbear one another	Eph. 4:2
Forgive one another	Eph. 4:32
Comfort one another	I Th. 4:18
Edify one another	I Th. 5:11
Exhort one another	Heb. 3:13
Consider one another	Heb.10:24
Have peace with one another	Mark 9:50
Know we are of one another	Rom 12:5
Same care one to another	I Cor. 12:25
Submit one to another	Eph. 5:21
Do not speak evil of another	James 4:11
Do not lie to another	Col 3:9
Don't hold grudges to another	James 5:9
Confess faults to another	James 5:16
Pray one for another	James 5:16
Have compassion one to another	I Peter 3:8

Friendship Frenzy and Fizzle

When do you know it's time to end a friendship? Not

every friend is meant to be our "best friend" and not every friendship is meant to last forever. These choices cannot be made lightly or callously, but hanging onto an unhealthy friendship too long is not good for either party involved.

Proverbs 17:17 says that "a friend loves at all times, and a brother is born for adversity." True friends love unconditionally, but unconditional love does not always mean unconditional approval. Overlooking "faults" in our friends is the admonition of I Peter 4:8 "...Love covers a multitude of sins." Yet, within most friendships there comes a time of conflict or confrontation.

Some friendships don't make it through the rough spots. They fizzle. Almost by mutual consent, strained friendships end. Particularly if you have a friend who subtly undermines your self-esteem or one who dumps all her troubles on you without caring about your needs, it might be time to consider a healthy way to end the friendship.

I've had to do just that. A number of years ago I was faced with such a problem. I wanted the friendship to work so badly that I hung in there hoping the other person would change. It was painful, especially since I was dealing with an emotionally fragile individual.

She was a woman with similar aspirations. We gave each other support and advice; we lunched together and attended our children's functions. I began to notice the strains due to jealousy on her part. In and out of my presence comments were made ... she began to be critical, cutting, comparing everything my children or I did.

Gradually, I quit sharing joys or accomplishments with her. Our visits began to feel more obligatory than absorbing. We saw each other less and less ... now it's even awkward to run into each other in the grocery store.

Yes, it hurt. I felt like I'd failed and must have asked myself a hundred times what I might have done to have salvaged the relationship. Yet, I knew I had to withdraw from a friend who meant so much to me in the past. We had entered a new era... it was time to part. After confronting this dear woman prayerfully, I came away a better person. I had never known anyone before to be jealous of me. That green-eyed monster will ruin any friendship. Envy diminishes both parties; it hurts the victim and leaves a bitterness in the heart of the perpetrator. It rots a person's bones (Prov. 14:30)!

A somewhat different experience happened when an acquaintance chose to exclude me. You know the type. She masqueraded as my friend. This rose ended up having lots of thorns. She constantly brought me gifts, called daily and insisted on buying when we were out to eat. If we went out to lunch or antique shopping, she insured the whole church knew about our time together the next Sunday. And if, heaven forbid, I ever forgot to seek her out at any event, she became uncommunicative and pouty.

More and more I felt like this woman's "trophy" than her friend. I began to discern that ours was a one-way friendship which did not embody mutuality. Again, I was hurting. The friendship grew increasingly uncomfortable. One day I approached her, and asked her to explain why she was avoiding me. She answered, not confronting a specific behavior or incident, but attacked me as a person, my whole identity.

I set myself up for the pain (I have a tendency to depend more on my human relationships than God). This was a reminder to be dependent on God alone. Risky, too risky.

"But, God..." I pleaded relentlessly with the Lord, praying the verses in Psalms chapters 55, 56, 57, 59, 60, and 64. (David knew what it felt like to be betrayed by one whom he had trusted). "Lord, every day she wrests my words, she gathers herself with others, they marred my steps, they wait for me to come by... their teeth are spears and their tongues are sharp swords ... their words are poison ... they run and prepare themselves without my fault, they bend down to shoot their bitter words like arrows at me ... I am wounded... for it was not an enemy that reproached me, then I could have borne it, neither was it her that hated me that did magnify herself against me; then I would have hid myself from her...But, it was her, one of my equal ...we took sweet counsel together, and had walked into the house of God together..."

I poured out my heart as David of old. God knows me inside and out and cared about my deep hurting. His soothing balm healed my aching heart. I can still remember the date and time. On that day in my journal I glued the "Friends" bookmark that had graced my desk for months. I had not abandoned my friend; it was just a learning season for both of us.

The weeks passed, and so did my intense emotional pain when we chanced to meet. My *natural* inclination would be to not risk it again. Withdraw. Avoid. Stay at arm's length. Refuse to establish any close relationships. Yet, the gift of friendship is too precious and rewarding for that. How thankful I am that I have continued to find great camaraderie in many comforting friends since then.

A few years ago we were privileged to host Dee Brestin for the weekend. She says it well in her book, *The Friendships of Women,* "When a rose gardener is jabbed by a thorn, she realizes the rose had no personal animosity toward her but was simply born with thorns." And so, without restraint, I have reached out to embrace the gifts of friendship often. Unwrapping them, even now, I feel my soul watered by the sweet refreshing memories of their love.

Quilts Are Made With All Shapes and Colors

Women who lived during the colonial times ordered their lives around weekly gatherings to design quilts for the new brides. These "quilting bees" or "sewing circles" provided strong intergenerational ties. Older women wrapped their arms of kindness and wisdom around the younger women as they shared their lives through informal mentoring.

I have learned so much from older women. In our hurried, troubled world there is a call to return to a gentler time — a time when traditions, shared values, and kinship with an older woman provides a sense of safety and comfort. Somehow, mentoring gently imposes a confidence which helps any young woman maintain perspective in days filled with chaos. Her spirit is renewed, knowing there is "backup." "I have someone I can count on to be there for me!"

I had never experienced this kind of mentor—friendship outside of my family until Betty (she wasn't old, but she was older to me) asked me to come by her house with my two young daughters. While Missy and Mindy enjoyed a swim, I

observed Betty making preparations for her weekend enter-
taining. Having lived all over the world with her husband in
the military, Betty was a hostess extraordinaire! I wanted to
know how she did everything!

Our friendship flourished, and over the next six years I
grew in so many ways just by spending time with her. By
osmosis I picked up so much knowledge from this hospi-
table, godly woman. I learned how to place buffet items so
the flow will go smoothly, bathroom towel folds, gracious
luau decorations and authentic foods. Christmas ginger-
bread houses were her specialty. I never have guests to this
day, that I don't think of Betty who nurtured me in so many
ways. What a help her advice in hospitality has been for me
in serving as a pastor's wife.

Another mentor, who has literally been a beacon of light
in my life, is an older (certainly not old) pastor's wife. Mrs.
Gillming's personal behavior, ethics, unshakable faith, and
creativity has had a profound effect in my life. This dynamic
lady is eager to encourage younger, less-seasoned women.
Offering me invaluable advice and encouragement, she has
been a tremendous inspiration for this book's completion. I
would not be speaking and writing books today had she not
encouraged me to do more than I ever thought I could
possible do.

Perhaps you could find several mentors. One might excel
in raising children, another in hospitality, another in Bible
knowledge, and still another in a hobby or career you're
pursuing. Having a composite of mentors helps us all develop
to our fullest in many areas. We all need someone to believe
in us and encourage the potential out of us!

A mentoring relationship is obviously invaluable to a
younger woman, but it can be equally rewarding to the older
woman. My mother is especially amazing in that she be-
friends women of all ages. Younger women flock to her
because of her godly example and fun-loving spirit. Whether
at church or as a retired elementary teacher, she is always
involved in informal mentoring and sometimes doesn't even
know it. Everytime I have the opportunity to go to my folks'
church, I am amazed at the women who have gained invalu-

able wisdom from being with her or observing her. They tell me how blessed I am to be her daughter ... and I heartily agree!

Stitching the colors and shapes from many women's lives has quilted delightful bonds of friendship for me. Beautiful patterns have emerged. I appreciate the value of making myself vulnerable to other women. It has been in the drawing from many friendships of all ages that the Lord has helped me to see, "That's the kind of woman I want to be." And in the years that followed, I have tried to draw from their examples.

Older women (hmmm... I'm including myself now in this group) need to be mentoring, not just finding a mentor for ourselves. It is not optional. Scripture commands it in Titus 2:4. We will always be older to someone. Most of what I am today I learned from the older women in my life. Now it is a sincere joy to teach those things to my daughters and other women God puts in my life.

Are you approachable for younger women to ask for your help in their struggles? Gray hair, a matronly figure, or feeling "behind the times" should not prevent us from being there for younger women. Nurture a teachable spirit in yourself first, then pass down your learning to future generations.

I think you'll find all women have much in common. We're not so very different when it comes right down to it. Young parenting women are experiencing the very same difficulties we were facing just a few short years ago, if not now; sex, careers, relationships, time management, homemaking, childbirth, etc.

Don't wait until you're old and gray. It is time for us who are in our forties and fifties to begin being responsible for the commands in Titus 2, "to teach the younger women to love their husbands and their children." You could begin by initiating a friendship. Send an encouraging card. Find something in common. Perhaps you have walked in her shoes. An illness that you have survived such as cancer or a loss of a child would naturally draw you to a younger woman who is experiencing similar fears.

With so many women living away from extended families, we must keep our doors of friendship always wide open.

You never know who God might bring your way to befriend you. God often brings women to walk through my door just when I feel I can't juggle the pressure any longer. They relieve me of responsibilities in my home and ministry so that I can concentrate on the major issues of my life and not be sidetracked. Their lending supportive hands help to refuel my creativity, energy and productivity.

"Minimum Daily Adult Requirement"

Does the deepest part of your soul ache today for a special friend? Maybe you have division in your family. Is your "house divided" with family members who have not spoken to each other in years? Are you afraid to step out and risk again after betrayal in a past friendship? Does someone need an apology from you?

God has a better plan. YOU be the one to restore strained relationships. Write a letter, make the phone call, hug for just a hug's sake — whatever it takes. Think of how you would like to be treated by others and treat them that way! Reach out and assure people in your life that they are loved by you. Buy a book of "love" postage stamps and write uplifting notes to some friends today. Does your special friend have a theme (gardening, angels, teacups, lambs)? Send her a little gift to show your love.

To have friends, you must show yourself friendly! Friends are like a beautiful scent — they bring joy to the heart! (Prov. 27:9) After I am with my friends memories of our time together surround me with the beautiful fragrance of their love. I myself feel more beautiful and am motivated to reach out to others in love.

Because my office is in my home, I miss the interaction of coworkers. I schedule "breaks" to pick up the phone just to share a word with a friend and hear a voice on the other end so I don't lose touch with people. During yesterday's pressure-packed day, my "break" included taking the short drive down to our church. In the brief visit with our two secretaries, I laughed, brainstormed, and came away rejoicing. Both ladies reassured me that they love and support me. Their touches were such an encouragement in my day!

Last week, I met Linda for a walk. She knows me inside and out. It's something wonderful we share — we are to each other an extension of ourselves, like "second selves." We couldn't count the times we've been asked "Are you two sisters?" We giggle and always say the same phrase in unison, "No, but that's a compliment."

Yes, we are bonded close, but that doesn't mean we have to be always together. We may not sit together at meetings so that we can be open to other people whom the Lord puts in our paths. I am blessed with so many friends because of this. Good friends know they are soul mates but don't smother each other. Loosening a tight grip on a close friend gives freedom so both can grow without an unhealthy dependency. Most women I admire say they have several "best friends." That concept expresses a wonderful appreciation of giving space to one another — a sacrifice that strengthens any relationship in life.

Don't forget the gift of friendship at home! Tell each member of your family today that you love them and why. Tell God the negative things. Tell your family the positive things about themselves! We would cultivate better friendships right inside our homes if we would make it our job to keep our family happy ... and let God make them holy.

We women are clearly the thermostats of our homes. When we are warm, others take on the same temperature. Be a warm, good friend to your husband today. When he comes home from a tiring day at the office, be his friend. Those first few moments set the tone for the rest of the evening. Let him catch his breath and rejuvenate. Don't unload on him about all that went wrong in your day. Offer him something to drink and keep the children somewhat settled until Dad can regroup.

Do your children feel loved by you? I see so many women burning the candle at both ends that they hardly know their own children. Proper parenting takes love and time. It's not a hit-and-miss experience. Friendships will not flourish if we neglect the key ingredients of cultivating, nurturing, and proper care.

Children left to themselves, like gardens, will not

produce a bountiful harvest. They will just grow weeds. Proper pruning is necessary for a "crop" that is satisfying and rewarding. Give your child the precious gift of TIME today! Eyeball to eyeball, stop and listen to them. What an awesome friendship will begin to develop!

Some days I forget to take my vitamins. If I forget too many days in a row, I begin to notice a sluggishness. I am withered by two in the afternoon. This is the same with intimacy. I've discovered I can go for a whole day, even a few days, without the energizing of intimate friendships. But no longer...soon I cease to grow. My roots dangle, branches droop, and leaves fall. I make sure to renourish with a friend before I wither and die!

As someone once said, "Cast your bread upon the waters and it will come back to you buttered!"

Take Advantage of Coupons, Not People

I faithfully clip coupons out of every Sunday paper. Do I always follow through? Not on your life! Do my coupons get redeemed? Not many. Most of them end up in a drawer or stuffed in my purse until the expiration date is long past. Oh, my motives are good. I intend to use them, yet somehow I just never get around to it.

Being a good friend requires a similar discipline. Repeatedly in Scripture we see friendship patterns that include an unfailing love and loyalty. The very nature of God is love. Elizabeth blessed Mary when she shared fears at hearing the angel's tidings. "Blessed is she who has believed that what the Lord has said to her will be accomplished!" (Luke 1:45). Naomi thanked Ruth and Orpha, "May the Lord show kindness to you, as you have shown to your dead and to me" (Ruth 1:8).

Like Christ, Who shows us His faithfulness when we are in need or hurting, we must respond with help and kindness to the hurting. Will you befriend the hurting and unlovely, despite the sacrifice it may require on your part? Who might the Lord be bringing across your path for you to help? Are you too preoccupied in your own affairs to notice?

Take time to read the story in Luke 10:25-37. Put your

name in place of the priest in verse 31. Not a good story, is it? Read it again and this time put your name in place of the Levite in verse 32. Still does not sound good. Lastly, put your name in place of the man who was hurt in verse 30. How do you like the story now? How do you feel about the two friends who went on by?

Lastly, put your name in place of the good Samaritan. Do you feel better with this version of the story? Of course you do! That man was a friend. He was alert to someone in need, lifted him up, overcame obstacles, and showed God's love. May we do the same! Reach out and take opportunities to show love to hurting, bleeding people God brings across our path, and not just pass them by.

Making friends doesn't come easy for you? Notice these principles to use in reaching out to others taken from *How to Win Friends and Influence People* by Dale Carnegie.

Here are six easy things to remember:

1. Become genuinely INTERESTED in people.

2. SMILE (have one ready for everyone you meet).

3. Remember that a person's NAME is the sweetest sound to the ears. It shows you care enough to take note of them.

4. LISTEN more and speak less. Encourage others to talk about themselves.

5. Talk about the other person's INTERESTS rather than your own.

6. Make the other person feel IMPORTANT in sincere ways.

The point is, perspective is all about HOW we choose to see others. Each person is a potential friend. What a gift! So, untie the ribbons — encourage, listen, share time, smile, show concern, and a hug!

I never pass a teddy bear in a gift shop without longing to hold or cuddle it. They just seem to reach out and say, "Hug me!" So I do! Yours and my friends are much the same. Similar to teddy bears, the older they get, the more they're worth! Let's go ahead and make their day. Hug 'em and let 'em know how much they're loved!

Power of Prayer

I got up early one morning and rushed into the day; I had so much to accomplish that I didn't have time to pray.

Problems just tumbled about me and heavier came each task. "Why doesn't God help me? I wondered. He answered, "You didn't ask."

I wanted to see joy and beauty, but the day toiled on, gray and bleak; I wondered why God didn't show me. He said, "But you didn't seek."

I tried to come into God's presence; I used all my keys at the lock. God gently and lovingly chided, "My child, you didn't knock."

I woke up early this morning and paused before entering the day; I had so much to accomplish that I had to take time to pray.

—Author Unknown

Chapter 9

"The Gift of Leaning"
Untie the Ribbons of Prayer

One day this past winter, with my arms loaded with packages, books and holiday decorations, I carefully made my way from the garage up our icy deck steps. You guessed it! Sliding open the glass door, I lost my balance, and fell inside, dropping everything onto the kitchen floor. Upon examining the damage, I found all to be in order except my brand-new Este Lauder compact I had just purchased.

It looked fine on the outside, but inside the powder and glass were shattered in a million little pieces. Looking at the mess, I thought, "Little compact, I identify with you. How many times I've felt just like you look...shattered!"

Coming Unglued

After a great fall, is there anything or anyone who can put us "Humpty Dumptys" back together again? When your husband's remarks cut like a knife, who gives you the stamina to keep on going? When you are overwhelmed as daily pressures mount, who gives you the strength to have a relaxed mental attitude? When you just want to pop one of your children for spoiling your plans, who gives you the power to have self-control?

He is God. Let Him handle your falls, disappointments,

and pain. No matter how "together" on the outside you may look, your inside may be fragmented and shattered. By receiving the greatest gift of all (at Christmastime, I love to save the best till last) you can be more than just glued back together ...you can be transformed!

From my earliest recollection of my childhood, I recall knowing that God loved me and had a wonderful plan for my life. I knew God is love and could quote John 3:16 as a youngster, "For God so loved the world that He gave His only Begotten Son, that whosoever believeth in Him should not perish, but have everlasting life."

God's love was for me! For God so loved "Sharon" — I could put my name right in that verse. Everlasting life offered to me? Wonders of wonders! Then, reading the same chapter (verse 34), I found abundant life was available. That sounded really good to me. Well, what was keeping me from this gift? I came across a list of "iniquities," sins, that were keeping me from God and His power in my life. They weren't gross sins like murder or robbery, but I identified just the same with worry, unbelief, pride, gossiping, self-will, etc.

That was me. Sin was separating me from God. My emptiness and devastating loneliness was because of sin. There was more. I read that the penalty for my sin is death... spiritual death. "For all have sinned and come short of the glory of God" (Romans 6:23). "Oh, no" ....I remember thinking. "I'm a goner!"

"That's me, I am a sinner," I groaned, "I'll never have eternal life or experience God's love for me." Well, enough of the bad news. The good news was that Jesus Christ made provision for my sin. Romans 5:8 says, "But God commendeth his love toward us, in that, while we were yet sinners, Christ died for us." For me ...for you! Whoa, that changed the whole picture.

I eagerly read on. Jesus' life was one of unselfishness, even unto His impending death. Because He died, I could live. He was symbolically knocking at the door of my heart, "Behold, I stand at the door, and knock: if any man hear my voice, and open the door, I will come in to him, and will sup with him, and he with me" (Rev. 3:20).

It wasn't enough just to know these truths. I needed to open that door, reach out, and receive this free gift! "But as many as received him, to them gave he power to become the sons of God, even to them that believe on his name" (John 1:12). Oh, how I wanted to have what God was offering to me. I could hardly wait to do it!

"For by grace are you saved through faith; and that not of yourselves; it is the gift of God. Not of works, lest any man should boast" (Eph. 2:8,9).

Receiving God's free gift involves turning to God from self in repentance. It is an act of the will, not dependent on feelings or anything I might attempt to do for myself. I prayed silently, "Dear Lord Jesus, I believe You died on the cross for me. I invite You into my life and receive You as My Savior and Lord. Thank you for forgiving my sins and giving me eternal life. Take me completely and make me the person You want me to be. Thank you. Amen."

Does this prayer express what you are searching for in your life? You, too, can accept this free gift... not to be reformed, but transformed because of the promises of God. To invite Jesus Christ into your life, simply open the door. Place your trust in the trustworthiness of God. He is wanting and waiting to fill the vacuum in your heart. This wonderful gift is yours for the asking! I've never been sorry, and neither will you.

Right now you can become a Gifted Woman in every true sense of the word. Your life can have peace, power, pardon and purpose. The Bible promises that you will become a new person inside and an abundant new life will begin! I hope you will invite Him to come in. God is waiting and wanting you to simply open your heart's door and tell Him so. The prayer that I prayed has been used as a suggested prayer in many of my classes.

The Awesome Difference This Gift Makes

Since that all-important day, just as there are certain privileges I can enjoy because I am my parents' child, wonderful benefits are mine to enjoy by becoming a child of God (John 1:12). The first benefit is **peace** from God Himself who is the Prince of Peace. Peace is deep-down in my heart. "...my peace I give unto you..." (John 14:27).

Secondly, **power** to live the abundant life is available to me as a child of God. Power to transform my flawed natural love for others into a divine love — supernatural from God Himself because Jesus came into my life (Colossians 1:27).

Thirdly, I received **pardon** since Jesus paid the penalty for my sins. All I ever did or ever will do wrong has been forgiven (Colossians 1:14). I am acquitted, set free, a truly liberated woman.

Lastly, I now know I have true **purpose** in life. Jesus *is* "the way, the truth, and the life." My relationship with Christ assures me that He will never leave me nor forsake me (Heb. 13:5). On the basis of His promises, when I received Christ, I began the great adventure for which He created me (John 10:10 and 2 Cor 5:17).

Don't "Come Out of the Closet"

I heard the saying once, "To grow tall in your faith, root your life in prayer." I've been learning that my functioning as Rob's wife, as a pastor's wife, or speaking, writing or mothering, should not become a substitute or replacement for prayer.

The greater the quality of our invisible private life spent in study, planning, and prayer, the more effective our visible life will be. Hidden times of shutting out the world each day will settle your heart with God and provide times of growing. For a time each day, even if it is just fifteen minutes, shut out the world! The Bible calls it "entering into your closet" (Matt. 6:6).

Your "closet" may be your desk, a private study or guestroom, under a tree, or on the back porch. Some young moms find that their only getaway is the bathroom! It's only there that they can lock the door and have some uninterrupted time!

The quality of your life will be determined by the amount of time you spend alone with God in reading, praying and planning. Remember how much time and planning it took to make your exquisite wedding go smoothly? Every detail was thought out and planned for months. That's what makes an exquisite life! Everything is prayed over, planned, thought out behind the scenes ... well in advance of the actual events.

I have found that setting an actual appointment to meet with God the next day really helps me stay committed to a specific time. If one of us is not there, guess who is the "no show?" I don't dare stand up the Lord! Just "fitting in" my time with Him doesn't work for me. I need to settle my heart with God before the day begins with its constant interruptions, unexpected telephone calls and surprises.

My "closet" is not my office. There at my desk I am too easily distracted with my daytimer, phone, and the numerous tasks vying for my attention. I choose to sit with a cup of coffee, journal, and Bible in hand in my living room, which is seldom used except for company. In the solitude of this room I am not so distracted (except by occasional cobwebs that call for my attention).

In pretty weather I love to drive to a nearby lake or somewhere where I'm anonymous and sit on a blanket or park bench. Sometimes after everyone is breakfasted and off for the day, I love to treat myself to a quiet corner of a restaurant to sit, have breakfast, read and plan.

Seeking out occasional extended time-slots (I try to do this once a month) helps me to evaluate where I've been and where I'm going. Jesus did! He often slipped away from the crowd because He felt the need. Once that we know of, He spent an entire night in prayer (Luke 6:12).

Jealously guard your "closet time." Start with fifteen minutes a day — we can all give up that much sleep. Make the sacrifice! Everything else can wait if you are guided by this priority. Where do you want to be in five ... ten .... fifteen years? Unless you are rich in God, His Word and prayer, nothing will last of eternal significance.

Creative Journalizing

Writing out my prayers and actually praying Scripture has become a wonderful way of conversing with God. This has been the number one shot in the arm that my prayer life needed and has done more in the last five years to draw me closer to my Lord than anything I can remember! Surpassing anything I dreamed possible, my relationship with the Lord has been strengthened again and again. It's a lifetime process. I give God the thanks for His goodness to me over the years. How I praise Him for guiding me through times of pain, joys, struggles and hurts.

Somedays I have been experiencing a hurt or deep trial when I enter my "closet," but oh, the inner peace and tranquillity that comes from reciting and reading His Word! It helps me to lean on Him, to draw on His strength, and to learn to be like Him. Then I am free to reach out to others in love. God's Word is literally the foundation of my security and power source for life!

I think of a particular situation this past school year when I was especially distressed over a situation concerning Missy. Being over a thousand miles away from home while living at college, she handles life's responsibilities incredibly well. It is me, the mom, who doesn't always trust things will turn out okay. Long-distance parenting and releasing my grown children are not easy for this "hands-on-mom".

The best and most effective thing I can do for my children is to pray for them. It is a habit you need to develop before your children leave the nest. After your children have gone to sleep, go into their rooms, kneel beside them, and pray. Rare will be the times tears don't come! I go into my girls' rooms now just to pray and feel near them. The very bedspread my head leans on has their sweet smell and I feel close to them.

So you see, when Missy is hurting and my arms cannot hold her, I have discovered I must let God do the holding. Peace came when I prayed the Scripture Isaiah 41: 10 for her: "Father, give Missy a heart that really knows you are with her. Help her to fear not, for you are with her: to be not dismayed for you are her God. I know, Father, you will strengthen her. Yea you will help her. I trust that you are holding Missy with your right hand of righteousness."

Missy's situation did not change, yet I felt assured that she was safe just by turning her over to the heavenly Father's care. His promises in His Word are true. For three days I had yo-yoed up and down, burdened unnecessarily.

The prayer wheels began turning! It felt so good to let God hold onto Mindy as well. "Lord, today keep Mindy from the traps that may be set for her by evildoers. Let the wicked fall into their own nets, while she passes by in safety" (Psalms 141: 9, 10).

And for Rob, I prayed aloud while writing in my prayer journal, "Lord, I ask that today as Rob serves you, that you would let his light shine before the members in the flock you've given us to care for. May they see Rob's good deeds and praise his Father in heaven" (Matthew 5:16).

I've developed a love for praising God using my own wordings of Psalms and other Scriptures. Guess which one this is: "God, I thank you that your eyes are over the righteous, and your ears are open to my prayers. I praise you that you are near to me when I call upon you, to all that call upon You in truth. Thank you, Father, that you will fulfill the desire of them that fear you. You hear my cry and will save me." That's I Peter 3:12 and Psalm 145:18 and 19.

When your child wants a specific toy for his birthday, he doesn't beat around the bush, suggest or hint. He doesn't say, "Oh, anything is fine, just bless me with a blessing." No, he comes right out and asks! We are to pray specifically. We are to pray with childlike simplicity and trust (Luke 18:16,17).

"Pre-Monster Syndrome"

There are certain chunks of time in the month where I would like to P.M.S. — Pack My Suitcase! Just run away! What helps during this time is to rename this syndrome, "Pray More, Silly!" It is better for me and Rob. More time with my loving heavenly Father on days I am not so loving can make a big difference.

Prayer is more than coming to God with a shopping list full of your requests. I like to use the formula of ACTS:

A   adoration of God.

C   confession of sins, keeping short accounts.

T   thanksgiving, especially for answered prayer and praise for God's character and working in my life.

S   supplication for others, their needs, and longings
    of my heart.

Days when I'm especially a "monster," I bring my emotions before Him, praying Ephesians 6:13, "I pray that I will
put on your full armor, God, so that when the day of evil
comes, I will be able to stand my ground, after I have done
everything, to stand."

Or Colossians 1:10, "I pray, Father, that I may live a life
worthy of You and please You in every way, bearing fruit in
every good work."

Dear friend, the indescribable joy that you will experience in prayer transcends any trials you're experiencing. You
will begin to look forward to your "closet time" daily. Fill in
the blanks with your family members, your needs, praises,
and heart's desires.

The following are some sample Scripture-based prayers
to get you started. Have a great time developing your own
additions to these:

A Sample Scripture-Based Prayer

Father,
I commit my day to You.
I trust also in You and
You shall bring it to pass.
Psalm 37:5

Father, You will instruct me
and teach me in the way I should go,
You will guide me with Your eye.
You will give me the desires of my heart,
because I have delighted myself in You.
Psalm 32:8

Father, I will be kept in perfect peace today,
for I have chosen
to let my mind be "stayed" on You.
Make it a reality
in my life

as I trust in You.
Isaiah 26:3

Father, I thank You for sending angels
to prepare the way for me;
I thank You for favor for each hour's appointment
I thank You that I can choose LIFE and LOVE
and not death and sin.
I thank You for the armor I have on to protect me,
and I thank You that I am covered by the blood.
Ephesians 6:10-17
I John 1:7

Father,
I thank You that
I walk in newness of life
this day.
Romans 6:4

Praying Scripturally For our Children

Fill in the blank with your child or loved one's name!

"For _____ is transplanted into the Lord's own garden, and
is under His personal care."
Psalm 92:13

"Withhold not your tender mercies from _____, O Lord, let
your loving kindness and your truth continually preserve
_____."
Psalm 40:11

"That _____ will follow you, Lord, because he knows Your
voice. May he never (on any account) follow a stranger, but will
run away from him, because he does not know the voice of
strangers or recognize their call."
John 10:4-5

"Lord, Keep my _____ from the traps set for him by evil-

doers. Let the wicked fall into their own nets while he passes by in safety."
Psalm 141:9,10

"Don't let others spoil _____'s faith and joy with their philosophies, their wrong and shallow answers built on men's ideas, instead of on what Christ has said."
Colossians 3:8

"That _____ would hear the instruction of his father; and reject not nor forsake the teaching of his mother."
Proverbs 1:8

"I ask that you keep and protect _____ from the evil one."
John 17:15

"I ask that the worries of the world, and the deceitfulness of riches, and the desire for other things will not creep in and choke and suffocate the Word in _____'s life."
Mark 4:19

"O Lord God of our fathers; make _____ always want to obey you, and see to it that his love for You never changes. Give _____ a good heart toward God, so that he will want to obey You in the smallest detail."
I Chronicles 29:18

"That _____ would not be quarrelsome — fighting and contending, may he be kindly to everyone and mild-tempered — preserving the bond of peace."
II Timothy 2:24

"Let _____'s light shine before men, that they may see _____'s good deeds and praise his Father in heaven."
Matthew 5:16

Let's pray that our children will influence an ungodly world.

Prayer Suggestions

Praying For Your Children

Train a child in the way he should go, and when he is old he will not turn from it (Proverbs 22:6).

Pray for their relationship with God:

That they may know "how wide and long and high and deep the love of Christ is, and know this love that surpasses knowledge" (Ephesians 3:18, 19).

That at any early age they may accept Jesus Christ as their Savior (II Timothy 3:15).

That they will allow God to work in their lives to accomplish His purpose for them (Philippians 2:13).

That they will earnestly seek God and love to go to church (Psalm 63:1 and 122:1).

That they will be caught when guilty (Psalm 119:71).

Pray for Godly attributes:

That they will be protected from attitudes of inferiority or superiority (Genesis 1:27, Philippians 2:3).

That they will respect authority (I Samuel 15:23).

That they will hate sin (Psalm 97:10).

That they will be able to control their temper (Ephesians 4:26).

That they will exhibit the fruit of the Spirit in their lives (Galations 5:22).

Pray for family relationships:

That they will obey their parents in the Lord (Proverbs

1:8,9 and Colossians 3:20).

That they will accept discipline and profit from it (Proverbs 3:11,12 and 23:13).

That they will love their siblings and not allow rivalry to hinder lifelong positive relationships (Matthew 5:22).

That we as parents may so live before them as to entice them to the banqueting table, not drive them away (Matthew 5:16).

Pray for relationships with friends:

That they will choose Godly friends who will build them up in the Lord (Proverbs 27:9 and Ecclesiastes 4:10), and be kept from harmful friendships that will lead them astray (Proverbs 1:10).

That they will be firm in their conviction to withstand peer pressure (Ephesians 4:14).

That they will be a friend to the lonely, the discouraged, the lost (Matthew 25:40; Philippians 2:4).

Pray for protection:

From the evil one (John 17:15).

From drugs, alcohol, and tobacco (Proverbs 20:1 and 23:31,32).

From victimization and molestation (Luke 17: 1,2).

From premarital sex (I Corinthians 6:18-20).

From physical danger - accidents and illness (Philippians 4:6).

Pray for their future:

That they will be wise in their choice of a mate — pray

now for the one who will marry your son or daughter that they will be raised in a Christian home, remain pure, and that they will bring one another great joy (Proverbs 19:14). (And pray that you will be a good mother-in-law!!)

That they will be wise in their choice of a career (Proverbs 3:6).

That they will be wise in the use of their God-given gifts, talents, and abilities (Matthew 25:21).

Love the Lord your God with all you heart and with all your soul and with all your strength. These commandments that I give you today are to be upon your hearts. Impress them on your children. Talk about them when you sit at home and when you walk along the road, when you lie down and when you get up (Deuteronomy 6:6,7 NIV).

Special Prayer Promises

"Call to me, and I will answer you, and show you great and mighty things, which you know not" (Jeremiah 33:3).

"If you abide in me, and my words abide in you, you shall ask what you will, and it shall be done for you" (John 15:7).

"The effectual fervent prayer of a righteous man avails much" (James 5:16c).

"Again I say to you, that if two of you shall agree on earth concerning anything that they shall ask, it shall be done for them of my father which is in heaven. For where two or three are gathered together in my name, there I am in the midst of them" (Matthew 18: 19, 20).

"And whatsoever you shall ask in my name, that will I do that the Father may be glorified in the Son. If you shall ask anything in my name, I will do it" (John 14: 13,14).

"Likewise the Spirit also helps our infirmities; for we know not what we should pray for as we ought, but the Spirit himself makes intercession for us with groanings which cannot be uttered" (Romans 8:26).

"And all things whatsoever you shall ask in prayer, believing, you shall receive" (Matthew 21:22).

"Therefore I say to you, that whatsoever things you desire, when you pray, believe that you receive them, and you shall have them" (Mark 11:24).

"Hitherto have you asked nothing in my name; ask, and you shall receive, that your joy may be full" (John 16:24).

"And this is the confidence that we have in Him, that, if we ask anything according to His will, He hears us; and if we know that He hears us, whatever we ask, we know that we have the petitions that we desired of Him" (I John 5:14,15).

"For whoever shall call upon the name of the Lord shall be saved" (Romans 10: 13).

"And it shall come to pass, that before they call, I will answer; and while they are yet speaking, I will hear" (Isaiah 65:24).

"Let us therefore come boldly to the throne of grace, that we may obtain mercy, and find grace to help in time of need" (Hebrews 4:16).

"The Lord is near to them that call upon Him, to all that call upon Him in truth. He will fulfill the desire of them that fear Him; He also will hear their cry, and will save them" (Psalm 145:18,19).

"Be anxious for nothing, but in everything by prayer and supplication with thanksgiving let your requests be made known to God. And the peace of God, which passes all understanding, shall keep your hearts and minds through Christ Jesus" (Philippians 4: 6,7).

"For the eyes of the Lord are over the righteous, and His ears are open to their prayers, but the face of the Lord is against them that do evil" (I Peter 3:12).

"Ask, and it shall be given you; seek and you shall find; knock, and it shall be opened to you." (Matthew 7:7).

Celebrate the Gift

Pure and perfect are His gifts
Coming down from above;
Chosen with care, bought with a price,
Wrapped in our Father's love.
Let His people rejoice
With one heart, with one voice...

Come as you are to the Holy Child,
Son of God, Lord Most High.
Open your heart, you will receive
A gift you cannot buy.
Here is hope, ever new;
Let it be born in you.

Celebrate the gift of Jesus;
Celebrate the King.
Celebrate the gift of Jesus—
The reason that we sing.
O come, let us adore Him,
Lift our hearts in praise.
Celebrate the love of the Father;
Celebrate the gift of Jesus.

Recorded by
Twila Paris

Conclusion

The Great Gift Exchange

It is out of a great heart of love that God has bestowed upon us such cherished gifts! I am continually amazed at His generosity to me, just an ordinary person who is willing to be used for Christ's sake. His gifts are not only beautiful, they are powerful! Powerful enough to turn an ordinary lump of clay into a valuable, treasured vessel...a "gifted" woman!

Nostalgia washes over me as I reflect on the joyful gift-giving of holidays past. Our living room floor is covered with newly-opened presents amidst crumpled tissue paper everywhere. For me, the highlight of the day is when each family member expresses gratitude for the gifts received and for the love our family shares.

Praise emerges from my soul as I offer up a prayer of thanksgiving for these touching moments of unhurried, sincere reminders of God's faithfulness. I want to give something back to Him for all He has so graciously given me. Not to just reply with a polite "Thank you," but now it's my turn to reciprocate.

Because of God's blessings I have so much to give.

My rights, my health, my worries, my failures, my grown-up children, my husband...all gifts of value to the Lord. I wrap them up. They really belong to Him anyway. Like the popular card company slogan, I do care enough to send my very best! Isn't that what God gave to me! Jesus, His Son, his very best!

Wrapping it Up

My friend, thus far you have been on the receiving end. You have opened nine awesome packages of love! Now, you too, have a unique opportunity to give something back. Relinquish your ALL to Him. On the name tag of your heart, write, "To God With Love." Give Him a special gift that will affect the way you live. Give yourself your family problems, financial difficulties, broken heart, physical limitations, dreams deferred, prodigal child, doubts, fears . . . place them all one-by-one gently into a beautifully wrapped gift box. Close the lid very tightly. Then crisscross a pretty ribbon tightly around the box and tie it tight with your own heartstrings. Now place a lovely bow on top. This way, you won't be tempted to secretly remove any of the precious contents.

Unwavering, my dear one, entrust your cherished gift into the loving hands of Jesus. You must let go. Turn loose. Don't take it back, for it is a gift! Give without instructions...no "if onlys"...no receipt enclosed for a return to you. Your gift is safe in the arms of Jesus.

Now you can celebrate! The Lord will do "exceedingly abundantly more than we can ask or think" with anything or anyone you release to Him. In fact, nothing is truly secure until it is committed to our God. Need proof?

Look at Abraham. He unselfishly gift-wrapped Isaac, his most cherished possession, and surrendered him to God. It hurt; but by doing so, Abraham learned that everything is safe when committed to God. And what about that little lad who gave his lunch as a gift to Jesus? Oh, what a miracle he would have missed if he hadn't been willing to give!

Chances are, you've thought of many darkened areas of your heart that you could gift-wrap. No one can measure the impact of your gift exchange — expect blessings! You will find yourself nourished in body and spirit because you are no longer carrying around such heavy cares.

I am still hearing, months later, of blessings from women who wrapped their precious "heart gifts" for Jesus this past Christmas. Each woman in our group wrote one worry or heartache on a slip of paper, then placed it in an embellished gift box. Once the lid was sealed — gone were our concerns.

What a sweet spirit as three women led us in prayer, presenting our gifts to the Lord. You couldn't judge that package by its wrapping. On the outside it looked beautiful, but the inside was full of pain. We were grateful to go home, free of those heavy burdens! God accepted each and every one. We must immediately give ourselves afresh when we are tempted to take those things back. They are no longer our possessions.

That's when I am reminded, "Eye hath not seen, nor ear heard, neither have entered into the heart of man, the things which God hath prepared for them that love Him." Think of the most beautiful gifts you could ever imagine in your heart and mind. God is saying, *"Just wait! These are nothing compared to what I have for you to open for all eternity!"*

That's how God is — open one gift and there's more where that came from! Keep a fresh supply on hand so that you're always ready to celebrate. God's gifts are always just right for whatever the occasion — or no occasion at all.

You will find yourself in a new and exciting dimension, one where you become a sparkling, beautifully Gifted Woman!

Open them again and again!

RECOMMENDED READING

Building a Great Marriage
by Anne Ortlund (Revell)
Anne Ortlund shares the process of building a long, warm, close relationship: learning to "think two." Areas covered are: responsibilities, how to act like a husband or wife, the art of making up, commitment, outside relationships, jealousy and adjusting to babies.

Creative Romance
by Doug Fields (Harvest House)
Doug Fields offers more than 300 simple, fun ideas to bring romance back into marriage. Includes 50 "Date Your Mate" suggestions.

Fit to Be Tied
by Rev. Bill & Lynne Hybels (Zondervan)
The Hybels combine biblical precepts with reality to recommend creative ways to fortify a marriage relationship. Includes pointers on assessing the differences, resolving conflict, and parenting effectively.

The Gift of Sex
by Dr. & Mrs. Clifford Penner (Word)
A Christian guide to sexual fulfillment practically and frankly presented. Major attention is devoted to: the physical dimension of marriage, moving past sexual barriers, resolving difficulties, and finding help through counseling.

Hedges: Loving Your Marriage Enough to Protect It
by Jerry Jenkins (Moody)
The author exposes the precursors to infidelity and tells exactly how you and your spouse can protect your marriage.

Language of Love
by Gary Smalley & Dr. John Trent (Focus on the Family)
Introduces the concept of "emotional word pictures," which will capture your listener's attention instantly and multiply the impact of what you say by activating both the intellect and the emotions.

Lonely Husbands, Lonely Wives
by Dennis Rainey (Word)
The author gives practical tips on developing intimacy to prevent isolation and loneliness in marriage.

Seasons of a Marriage
by H. Norman Wright (Regal)
In this book, couples of all ages will discover the different stages of marriage they will encounter and how to prepare for the challenges they never thought about during courtship. Topics tackled are: expectations, affairs, healing of a marriage, mid-life crisis, empty nest, and death.

Straight Talk
by Dr. James C. Dobson (Word)
For every husband who wants to understand what it means to be a man, how he should relate to his wife, his role as a Christian father, his emotions and feelings about midlife, and his personal faith. Also for every wife who wants to better understand her husband.

Strike the Original Match
by Charles Swindoll (Multnomah/Questar)
A fresh, biblical look at God's original blueprint for marriage. Gives advice on how to rekindle and preserve your marriage fire. Includes chapters on debt, divorce, commitment, and the empty nest.

What Wives Wish Their Husbands Knew about Women
by Dr. James C. Dobson (Tyndale)
Identifies the ten main causes of feminine dissatisfaction and unhappiness in the marriage relationship. These are: absence of romantic love, in-law conflict, low self-esteem, problems with children, financial difficulty, loneliness-isolation-boredom, sexual problems, menstrual and physiological problems, fatigue-time pressure, and aging.

Love Must Be Tough
by Dr. James C. Dobson (Word)
Dr. Dobson addresses the phenomenon of disrespect in marital relationships and describes its role in the gradual drift toward divorce for millions of couples. This book is written not only for those on the brink of divorce, but also for anyone who seeks a better understanding of the complex interrelationship between men and women. Loving toughness can be applied to happy marriages to develop a healthy respect for each other.

Rekindled
by Pat & Jill Williams (Baker)
In this candid, personal account, a husband and wife share how the biblical principles of love can rebuild a crumbling marriage. Chapters cover confrontation, self-image, courtship, crisis, commitment, and long-term healing.

Your Marriage Can Survive Mid-Life Crisis
by Jim & Sally Conway (Thomas Nelson)
Describes the techniques for restoring and maintaining a healthy, intimate, mid-life marriage.

For more information regarding G.I.F.T.ed Women seminars, you may contact Sharon Hoffman at...

G.I.F.T.ed Women
P.O. Box 3044
Des Moines, Iowa 50316
(515) 289-1419
FAX (515)289-2743